BUSES

ANNUAL 1983

£3.95

Hay Lane Kingsbury
Preston Road Wembley
79
BURNT OAK BROADWAY
Liptons
Take a fresh new look at Liptons
The new flyover from London to Heathrow.
PAY DRIVER
MCW
BYX 251V

BUSES

ANNUAL 1983

Edited by Gavin Booth

LONDON

IAN ALLAN LTD

Acknowledgements

The photographs in Buses Annual 1983 were supplied by:
John Aldridge: 50-57
G. H. F. Atkins: 30-34
Gavin Booth: 112-116
Gavin Booth Collection: 128
Stewart Brown: 22, 23 (lower), 24, 25 (lower), 26 (upper), 28, 29
Stewart Brown Collection: 21
S. J. Butler: 16 (upper), 17
C. L. Caddy: 12
D. Clark: 89, 93 (upper)
G. Coxon: 94-96
Ian Cowley: 13, 107, 111
C. J. Davis: 46
Michael Dryhurst: 97-106
John E. Dunabin: 48
Courtesy Richard Febry: 77-79
D. Fereday Glenn: 88, 91, 93 (lower)
D. Fereday Glenn Collection: 90, 92
Mike Greenwood: 117-120
Greyhound Lines: 66, 67
Chris Howard: 6
Robert E. Jowitt: 35-41
David Kaye: 18, 19, 20
Kevin Lane: Back cover (bottom), 3
MAN-VW: 121
Alan Millar: 122, 123, 125, 127
G. R. Mills: 42-45
T. W. Moore: 80-87
Stephen C. Morris: 11
Moseley: 124
A. Moyes: 58-65
Adrian Pearson: 10
Courtesy Ribble Enthusiasts: 75
Courtesy S. Rigby: 74, 76
Ian Riley: Cover
Charles H. Roe Ltd: 23 (upper left)
C. J. Spring: 9
D. J. Stanier: 8
David Stuttard: 7
Volvo: 126
T. J. S. Whelan: 14, 15, 16 (lower)
D. G. Wilson: 27 (lower)
R. L. Wilson: 23 (upper right), 25 (upper), 26 (lower) 27 (upper), 68-73

Front cover: West Yorkshire PTE built up a large fleet of several hundred basically similar Roe-bodied Leyland Atlantean AN68/1Rs. This example is seen passing through Holme in spring 1980.

Back cover, top: Preserved Duple-bodied Bristol LL6B in Royal Blue livery.

Back cover, bottom: Leyland Atlantean of Brighton Corporation Transport seen wearing an overall advertisement.

Previous pages: Two generations of London Transport buses, seen on Burnt Oak Broadway during the RT Cavalcade in April 1981. Metrobus M251 passes green RT3148 and red RT4028, both preserved.

First published 1982

ISBN 0 7110 1231 8

Published by Ian Allan Ltd, Shepperton, Surrey; and printed by Ian Allan Printing Ltd at their works at Coombelands in Runnymede, England.

Contents

203 RUSHDEN

blended in South Wales
FROM ALL BRANCHES OF THOMAS AND EVANS

Coachwork by
ROBERTS
WAKEFIELD
ESTABLISHED 1856

Where Are We Now?

STEPHEN C. MORRIS

There are doubtless many deep-rooted causes for nostalgia. Nostalgia, it is said, isn't what it used to be; this is probably true, but it certainly seems that there is a lot more of it than once there was. It would seem that for whatever reason man has become less and less satisfied with what he's got or what life is and rather than looking to a bright future he has turned in on himself and started yearning for the 'good old days'. Sorry to get all philosophical; I suppose I'm as guilty as the next man when it comes to nostalgia, and it seems to be a characteristic of all people interested in transport.

My own memories don't stretch back that far, in fact. Most of them are centered on my native north-west England and I can't claim to remember such exciting things as Manchester Pilcher cars or Ribble Tiger TSs. Despite that, the vehicles of my youth are now superseded by a totally new generation; the Crosville Bristol Ls on which my earliest bus rides were carried out have long since gone, and so have even the Manchester Leyland PD1s and PD2s which took me to school. To look at the current breed of London Transport and London Country Leyland Nationals which are virtually the sole buses in my recently-adopted Home Counties domicile, those days of back-loaders in multitudinous hues which adorned the Manchester area seem a long time ago. I think, on balance, buses probably were more interesting then, but I have to confess that I quite *like* our local Nationals, even if they do sound as if the engine is trying to jump out every time they accelerate away from the bus stop outside my flat.

What started these nostalgic musings was mulling over a copy of that first volume by the editor of *Buses Annual,* an entertaining tome by the name of *Bus Stop.* That august literary offering was published by Ian Allan in 1969 and included an article by its compiler under the title 'Then there were nine.' He wasn't referring to green bottles or anything like that, but to the UK chassis manufacturers, which then included amongst their ranks such evocative names as AEC, Guy, Albion and Daimler as well as Bristol, Ford, Bedford, Leyland and Seddon. It is interesting now to look back over the last 13 years or so and see how things have developed.

How simple things were in 1969! Bus manufacture was solidly body-on-chassis, and it was easy to tell who was and who wasn't making chassis for buses. Also conspicuous by their absence were foreign manufacturers. At the time of writing this article, it would be impossible to borrow the title of Mr Booth's article and just stick an appropriate number on the end. Somehow, 'Then there were about seven plus a goodly number of importers' just

Left: Leyland's present double-deck chassis is the Olympian, now built at Bristol. It has already replaced the Fleetline and VRT and will ultimately lead to the end of Atlantean production. The first one to see service was Ribble 2100, with ECW bodywork.

Right: Whilst the predominant feature of the British bus manufacturing industry over the last decade and a half has been that of change, one or two things have stayed static. There is little apparent difference between this 1965 Alexander-bodied Daimler Fleetline *(above),* which was new to North Western as 167 (seen here in its later guise as Selnec (Cheshire) 4167) and this 1981 example *(below),* MRF160 in the Alexanders (Midland) fleet.

doesn't have the same ring about it. Why the confusion? Well, just what has happened to the Foden-NC project? And is Seddon producing the Pennine VII or isn't it? Is Bristol Bristol or is it Leyland? And so it goes on.

One common feature of the situation then and now is the name Leyland. In 1969 British Leyland had recently been formed, and Gavin Booth made the logical prediction that the names AEC and Daimler would remain on the bus side, with Leyland, Guy and Albion remaining for trucks. Given the tremendous reputation that both those manufacturers had on the bus side, this was not at all an unreasonable assumption. As we now know, it was not to be. The promising rear-engine Routemaster had been strangled at birth (even though at the time of writing the prototype FRM1 is still alive and kicking and hasn't even burst into flames for quite a few years), leaving AEC with no double-decker. It did still have the Reliance of course, which was the basis for a very powerful and refined coach. Although this AEC design had been around for a fair few years, it had developed into probably about the best underfloor-engined British coach of its time. However, by 1979 the unthinkable happened; Southall closed. No more AECs were there to be, and as a stop-gap the ZF six-speed gearbox found its way into the Leopard to try to appease AEC customers. With a few exceptions, it didn't. By that time, Daimler, virtually the oldest automotive name, had also gone from the bus world. The Coventry works which had produced some magnificent vehicles, the early ones having that superb fluted radiator, was closed and Fleetline production was transferred to Leyland in 1976. Somehow, Leyland Fleetline sounded most incongruous; can you imagine a Daimler Atlantean, or an AEC Titan? Surrealist in the extreme! Thus had ended two highly significant chapters in the bus history.

The last vestiges of Daimler continued with Fleetline production, which itself finished in 1981. The actual end of Fleetline production was surrounded with great mystery. Southend Transport was convinced it was having the last one (242; MRJ 242W, a registration

One of the recent success stories has been the Dennis Dominator, which has become quite a favourite with municipals. East Staffordshire 38 is typical of many with East Lancs bodies.

Right: Ribble's older Leyland Atlanteans had long lives. This 1962 PDR1/1, seen in 1976, had a Weymann 59-seat coach body.

which sounds far more like a Salford Atlantean), a belief which was furthered when one of the bodywork component suppliers issued a press release to that effect which was zealously taken up by the transport press. However, the 'Great Fleetline Mystery' (a film which Hitchcock never quite made) began when two more materialised for independent South Notts, which then stole Southend's thunder.

The two other Leyland-group manufacturers in 1969, Albion and Guy, did continue bus production as it happened for longer than AEC and Daimler, although like Daimler they lost their own titles in favour of Leyland. However, they continued to produce buses for overseas, and at the time of writing the rather basic front-engined Victory for African and other markets was produced at the former Guy works in Wolverhampton, but even that factory was threatened with closure.

This leads us to Leyland itself, and when reckoning up the number of chassis manufacturers Leyland provides us with more problems than most. Leyland's traditional works at the Lancashire town of the same name is still going strong and probably gives us the greatest continuity in the industry. Production of the two 'traditional' Leylands, the Leopard and Atlantean is likely to continue for the time being, but the end of the road must be in sight, as they are unlikely to be able to meet future noise regulations and their successors are now very much with us. Over its production run the Atlantean has gone from strength to strength; it started as a revolutionary concept in 1958 when it quite literally turned the industry back to front and has gone on to gain a reputation as a solid and dependable vehicle in the 1980s. Perhaps it will never generate quite the hallowed awe of the PD-series Titans (what could, we ask?) but the Atlantean will probably be the subject of some nostalgia, especially when its production run ends. Indeed the Atlantean is old enough already for some nostalgia in certain quarters. I often find my mind drifting in all-too-rare idle moments to the days of rich maroon Atlanteans of Ribble going to such exotic places as Great Harwood and Oswaldtwistle. Some were still soldiering on in 1981, albeit in a less flattering shade of pink (sorry, poppy red), but their more glamorous sisters, the Gay Hostess and White Lady coaches have long gone.

The Leopard is probably rather more of a curate's egg. Reliable it is, no doubt, and there is no denying it is fast – until the road starts ascending that is. Then the poor old driver usually has to sit back with his foot hard down and

165
BLACKPOOL
RIBBLE
1279
RRN 428

The Leyland Leopard has become the standard NBC coach chassis, but is beginning to show its age in certain respects. This West Yorkshire example, 2389, seen at Digbeth, Birmingham has Duple Dominant IV coachwork.

The hopes of the British coach industry are pinned on the Leyland Tiger, which so far seems to be living up to expectations. Scottish Bus Group is using a fleet of Tigers with Duple Dominant III bodywork on the London-Edinburgh route. Tiger prototype XH544 was used as part of the elaborate launch of this type in Tangier during 1981, hence the far from Scottish setting.

wonder if he'll be home for Christmas. Unfortunately, the noise, ride quality and in certain circumstances performance are not quite up to the standards required by modern coach operators (the AEC Reliance was better on all three counts), and this has been partly instrumental in the rise of foreign competition. Credit where it's due, though; the Tiger, which is the one new Leyland to be produced at Leyland, is a great improvement and should be able to 'claw' back some of the Leopard's lost ground.

That's really where the easy bit of talking about Leyland ends; do we count Leyland National or Bristol as Leyland or as separate manufacturers? In 1969, if one had mentioned 'Leyland National', the response would have been fairly blank; it was in 1972 that the now ubiquitous National emerged. It marked several radical departures from what had become traditional practice. Although the rear-engine single-deck concept had already caught on to an extent, such ways of doing things as integral construction and production line manufacture were new. For the first time operators had little say in the specification of vehicles they could order, other than a choice of lengths and single/dual doors. Mechanically a smallish turbocharged engine took the place of the traditional long-stroke, slow revving naturally-aspirated diesel which had been virtually the only way of doing things before. The driver was given all sorts of unaccustomed luxuries, and the basic National cab layout, now extended to the Tiger, Titan and Olympian models, still takes some beating ten years later. It was also the first wholesale application of air suspension, although others had tried it over many years, mainly on coaches. Ostensibly, the Leyland National plant at Workington is a joint venture, owned half and half by Leyland and the National Bus Company under the umbrella of Bus Manufacturers Ltd, but its policies do seem to be Leyland dominated. For example when Leyland was looking for a home for its nomadic Titan after the disasters leading to the closure of Park Royal it ended up at Workington, although NBC seems to have had no part in the development of Titan, which has, at the moment at least, become virtually a London Transport model. Like the National, Titan is of the new school, with air suspension and integral construction and from the public's point of view, one of its more impressive features is the very low noise level, but no doubt fleet engineers are less enthusiastic about the added complications brought about by such. Titan might well have had a more profound influence on the British double-decker had its production problems not set things back; in the event most of the early orders were cancelled and look like being lost for ever. Had that not been the case, it is probable that integral construction for double-deckers may have become virtually universal by now; in the event, the traditional body-on-chassis approach has made a comeback, albeit in a somewhat modified form.

Gavin Booth's comments about Bristol in 1969 are ironic in retrospect – he says that the company is '. . . really outwith the control of British Leyland . . .'' and 'Observers who are concerned with British Leyland's virtual monopoly are looking to Bristol to offer some keen competition . . .' In 1969, the situation was somewhat different – Leyland had only a 25% holding in Bristol and now it has 50%. Thus the traditional Bristol range is now decimated; apart from a few for certain very persuasive customers the highly esteemed RE range has departed this life; it was, it seemed, too strong a

competitor to the National. Also gone now is the VR, which probably only lasted as long as it did through becoming NBC's standard bus; it was not one of Bristol's more glorious creations. The LH too has been phased out, leaving Bristol producing Leyland buses in the shape of the Olympian and the export B21. When travelling aboard a somewhat glamorous MAN SR280 coach along the M4 recently, I found myself musing about the concept of rear-engine motorway coaches running on air suspension. What a shame, I thought, that the UK is incapable of producing such a vehicle. It is my privilege from time to time to ride on a 1967 Bristol RELH6G coach, and an even greater privilege to have been let loose behind the wheel on one occasion. Lo and behold, a British-built, rear engine air-sprung coach with a quiet, relaxed ride and a positively lethal performance! Here, without doubt, is an up-to-the-minute coach with world-beating potential; the only snag is we don't build it any more! Such is progress . . . .

Two manufacturers which haven't changed an awful lot since 1969 are Bedford and Ford. Traditionally the choice of the independent operator, they have made considerable inroads into larger fleets since 1969. Now that bus grant is almost gone, the use of lightweight for stage-carriage and express work is now less economic than once it was, and the lightweight boom of the 1970s has probably gone for good. Midland Red, it could be argued, started the trend around 1970, with a large order for Plaxton-bodied R192s. Unlike some specimens, they proved quite a good buy and lasted a number of years, some ending their days as those curious, cut-down minibuses. Really, the R-series Ford has not changed much over the years; it still has the engine up front, although the tell-tale hump has now vanished; by dint of leaning the engine over a bit it was possible to hide it under the floor. The Ford R-series has its origins in the D-series truck, which is probably appropriate as the first Ford buses were based on Model T trucks. The Ford has its place on certain types of stage work, and is still well suited to shorter tour work, but long journeys at sustained speed can get a little wearing. Bedford has evolved over the years. Unlike Ford, Bedford moved the engine completely out of the way, under the floor, but unlike most other builders kept it standing up. Now that turbocharging is available, giving 206bhp, the Bedford is getting into the upper echelons of coaching at last. A sad aside during the period under review was that most radical Bedford yet, the JJL. This, for those who don't remember it, was a very smart, rear-engined integral midibus, but it never quite made the grade for reasons best known to its builder. The JJL could have moved Bedford into something very new had its problem been overcome.

The last of Mr Booth's nine which is still going strong – after a fashion – is Seddon, but just at the moment that company poses a bit of a problem, as it doesn't seem to be doing much. Since 1969 Seddon and Atkinson have merged, and after a very thin time during 1980/81, which hit most truck builders, seems to be enjoying some success on the freight side. At the time of writing its only bus chassis is the Pennine VII, which was the descendant of the earlier front-engined IV, but with a Gardner engine on its side under the floor. Scottish Bus Group fell for the type in a fairly big way, even mounting some of its top-link M-type bodies on that chassis. Just at the moment SBG has none on order, and none seem to be in build, but rumour hath it that it is poised to rise up,

Arguably one of the finest coach chassis produced in this country in recent years was the Bristol RELH. However, this fine specimen, with ECW coachwork, Royal Blue 2365, is now preserved and the type is no longer produced.

In suspended animation at the time of writing, the Seddon Pennine VII, at that time the only Gardner underfloor-engined psv. Eastern Scottish ZS888 carries Alexander T-type 49-seat bodywork suitably adorned for use on the successful Edinburgh-Glasgow shuttle.

Phoenix-like, in a package with Willowbrook bodywork. Probably the outcome of that venture will be better known by the time this is read.

The pattern of a steadily declining number of UK chassis manufacturers has reversed in an unexpected way during the 1970s. Firstly, we find MCW entering agreements with the Swedish manufacturer Scania to produce complete vehicles, and then we find a new name emerging. The Ailsa company, based in Scotland, has had a greater effect on the British automotive scene than perhaps we give it credit for, as it was the first importer of Volvo trucks into the UK, starting in 1967. The company was started by Jim McKelvie and based in Barrhead. It worked closely with Volvo to produce multi-wheel variants of Volvo trucks for the UK market and in 1970 design work began on a front-engine double-deck underframe. In 1972 the organisation moved to the present Volvo plant at Irvine and a year later the first complete Ailsa was built and shown at the Scottish Motor Show of 1973. Although it had a Volvo engine, it was strictly a British design. Since then, the Ailsa – or Volvo B55 (as the bus was built at the Volvo factory in Irvine it became the Volvo B55 during the later 1970s, but home market examples reverted to the Ailsa name in 1980) has represented the only alternative to a rear-engine double-decker in the UK. It is a relatively uncomplicated machine and was built for semi-integral construction with Alexander bodywork. More recently, however, it has been bodied by Northern Counties and also by the short-lived Belgian-Irish alliance of Van Hool-McArdle which produced an attractive body for South Yorkshire PTE. The Ailsa has enjoyed a steady market, mainly in Scotland, although most of the English PTEs have tried it in varying numbers. It has also become quite a successful export.

As mentioned above, MCW had changed its role from that of bodybuilder to the building of complete vehicles using Scania BR111 running units. However, the end of that venture heralded a new, all-British, double-decker in the shape of the Metrobus. The Metrobus was basically an integral vehicle, although underframes could be bodied by other manufacturers if required. The prototype Metrobuses emerged in 1978, and led to the end of MCW bodybuilding as such, although it was rumoured in 1981 that MCW may well have to return to the bodybuilding field as orders for the Metrobus had become somewhat less prolific due to its main customer, London Transport, placing its 1981/2 order with Leyland for Titans. The success of the Metrobus in its first three years of production was quite remarkable. It could be said to have been due to the fact that the industry's appetite for advanced, integral double-deckers on air suspension with

encapsulated engines for reduced noise level and automatic transmission with integral retarders (sounds like a list of ingredients for Bird's Dream Topping!) had been whetted by the promise of the Leyland Titan, and the suspension of Titan production caused them to turn to MCW to fulfil their desires. As a result large numbers of Metrobuses found their way into the PTE and LT fleets, plus those of several municipalities and three NBC subsidiaries. It is arguable that MCW should have spent a bit longer developing the Metrobus before launching it in large numbers, but with an unexpected gap in the market and fleets anxious for such vehicles one can hardly blame the company for grasping the orders that were going. In the event, further development of the suspension and attention to noise level might not have come amiss.

One manufacturer which was conspicuous by its absence in 1969 was Dennis, a long-established bus producer but one that had decided to concentrate on its other interests after cessation of Loline production in 1967. Indeed, the Loline had lasted longer than intended due to several large orders appearing after the decision had been taken to drop the range. The reluctance of certain parts of the industry to let the Loline go quite so easily was probably explained by *Commercial Motor's* findings when road testing the bus in January 1963; it proved to be the most economical bus tested since World War II. The new Hestair Dennis range can now claim to be the most diverse in the country, and has been based on the increasingly old-fashioned policy of giving the customer what he wanted. Indeed it was dissatisfaction with the amount of available choice which would appear to have led to Dennis's first new model, the Dominator. This has been followed by front-engined export models, the Jubilant and Dart, a rear-engine range for double- or single-deck applications with simplified drivelines (the Falcon range) and most recently an underfloor-engine single-deck chassis, reviving another old name, the Lancet. So far, the Lancet has been built as a rural-service bus, but a premium coach with air suspension looks highly probable from the same range. At first it was wondered whether the Dennis revival would be little more than a flash in the pan, but it has now been accepted that Hestair Dennis means business and the range is enjoying an enviable reputation. It appears to have been a successful blend of modern technology and traditional philosophy.

The other new phenomenon of the 1970s and 1980s has been the upsurge in imports, described in detail by Alan Millar on page 123. One of the few conclusions to which one can come is that there is still room for variety in the bus world, which must be good news for the bus enthusiast. It is, as they say, an ill wind that blows nobody any good, and it is ironic, perhaps, that attempts to standardise the bus industry into one or two types manufactured by one concern have led us back to a situation where the range of buses available is ever-widening. So perhaps we can take heart by the thought that some things are as they used to be. In fact with London Transport wondering what it's going to replace its indestructable RMs with on central area services, and looking at the prospect of a new front-engined bus with a rear platform for crew operation, who knows? But I'll only believe that when it happens!

Buses from Above

Photographs by T. J. S. WHELAN and S. J. BUTLER

Above: One of Reading Transport's 'Jumbos' – 50 big Bristol VRT/LL6Gs with Northern Counties 76-seat two-door bodies delivered between 1971 and 1976. It is seen in Oxford Road, Reading, in 1978.

Left: On the Spa, at Scarborough in July 1979, a former Southdown Leyland Titan PD3/4 of 1965, with 69-seat forward-entrance Northern Counties body, in service with United.

From the somewhat depleted ranks of London Transport's SM family, SMS362, a 1971 AEC Swift 4MP2R with Park Royal 33-seat body, seen at Uxbridge in 1979.

The familiar shape of the fast-disappearing Bristol FLF, seen from an unfamiliar angle. Eastern National 2902, a 1967 FLF6G with 70-seat Eastern Coach Works body, seen in 1980 in sylvan Southend, about to dive under the Victoria Centre.

Sweeping down the fast lane at Uxbridge in 1979, a Green Line AEC Reliance with Plaxton coachwork on the 727 service.

On transfer duties at London's Heathrow Airport, a Willowbrook-bodied Ford R1014 of the Whyte's Airport Services fleet, seen in 1980.

Unashamedly box-like, London Transport T48, a 1979 Leyland Titan TNLXB2RRSp with Park Royal body, glimpsed from Romford Station in 1980.

All Shapes and Sizes

DAVID KAYE looks at an often overlooked – but frequently necessary – aspect of bus travel: the humble shelter.

Above: A study in wood, prefabricated concrete sections and tiles, at Pidley, Cambridgeshire.

Nobody seems at all certain when the first bus shelter was erected, or indeed any similar structure for the use of tram passengers, but a date around the turn of the present century ought to be a reasonably accurate guess. Stage carriages, stage waggons and country carriers' carts all used inn yards, with their accompanying covered accommodation. When George Shillibeer began his famous first stage carriage omnibus route from The Bank to Paddington in 1829 would-be customers hailed it at any point along the route, and probably never expected anyone to trouble about whether they were battered by the elements, whilst they were waiting for the welcomed appearance of the trio of horses pulling the conveyance. Indeed until it became necessary to allocate definite stopping places, in order to avoid even more congestion that was already present in late Victorian London, there seemed to have been little point in suggesting the location of any shelters at all.

Few of the original shelters survive today, although down in Brighton there are several cherished examples along Ditchling and Dyke Roads. Those along the former thoroughfare have been used successively by Brighton Corporation tramcars, trolleybuses and motorbuses (including the very first one-man-operated double-deckers on route 26A/46A in June 1966!). Nowadays the passengers wait for the Southdown VRs to descend down to the Aquarium. These shelters are substantial affairs made of seasoned wood and with glazed windows. One in Dyke Road has been partially encased in a nearby wall, but its future is jealously guarded by those who treasure such transport street furniture of a bygone age. In other areas wrought iron, favoured by the designers of the first public toilets, and usually painted in dark green, has escaped the clutches of the moderniser and the wartime scrap metal drivers, to afford creature comforts today.

The interwar period saw the mushrooming of rural routes, often started by an ex-serviceman with an ex-service vehicle. To serve such scattered communities, the cheapest form of protection was a small corrugated iron shelter placed at the end of the lane leading to a hamlet, like those at Cadwell, Great Tows and Withcall up on the Lincolnshire Wolds. In other places small, but neater, wooden huts appeared. Sometimes these were in a so-called rustic form, much in vogue during the 1930s, whilst others were made of creosoted, overlapping planks, full of splinters for the small boy who ran his hand along them!

By 1935 Bournemouth could boast of its double-decked bus station, together with its large, ornate bus shelter surmounted by a clocktower in the centre of the Square. But in my native Worthing, passengers had to take shelter in the Southdown's twin offices in South Street and Marine Parade. As a bus found a gap in the parked vehicles near either of these termini, people would fight their way out of the narrow doorways of the offices, and battle with each other to gain some of the limited seating on the bus. It was definitely the survival of the fittest – and this included determined old ladies armed with brollies! Then the Second World War brought its emergency regulations, so that in 1941 it was decreed from on high that six or more people waiting for a bus must form themselves into a queue – a most un-British conception. Now it is not pleasant to wait in an orderly line in the teeth of a force 9 severe gale along a seafront in December, so small pre-stressed concrete shelters were erected by each bus stop. These were alright for the passengers bound for Brighton, since their shelter took the full blast of the south-westerlies, but for the poor folks queueing for Angmering, Arundel and Bognor Regis, their shelters were facing the wrong way and it was the passengers who took the impact of the wind and the rain!

Meanwhile, inland in the London Transport area, the Underground was not the only place where you could find tubes. Flat-roofed, openwork shelters made up of steel piping sprang up from Whitehall to Woking, and from Marble Arch to Hemel Hempstead. Each had a timetable case with data on relevant routes – an optional extra ignored by many operators.

Advances in all kinds of technology are often faster under wartime pressure, and building materials are no exception. In particular research into prefabricated structures brought a whole new generation of shelters into existence. When I have given lectures in vernacular architecture, my starting point has often been to show a class slides of the various bus shelters along the former Lincolnshire Road Car route 61 (now 561/504) between Louth and Boston. These consist of a variety of designs and basic elements, including breeze blocks, aluminium/glass, prefabricated concrete section and a trio of unusual triangular wooden sectioned erections, each having a tree growing up its centre! One of these is more recent that the others, and was built at Sibsey, when a short stretch of by-pass isolated the main shelter in the village.

This highlights one of the tragedies of these interesting little buildings. When in October 1980 Lincolnshire replaced Louth town route 46 with a more frequent and comprehensive route 49, it was discovered that on its circuit of the north-east side of town the new bus shelter in Lime Grove was now on the wrong side of the road. Obviously the MAP planners had not realised this vital fact. So, on the initiative of the local drivers, that section of the 49 (now 549) route was quickly reversed in direction! Thus the countryside is littered with useless and unused shelters. Others see life only once a week, like the one opposite the Mad Cat at Pidley in Cambridgeshire, which is served by United Counties on Mondays only at 09.30hrs. (into St. Ives) and at 1233hrs. (into Ramsey).

Sometimes shelters stand out like sore thumbs in the landscape, but in other places great care has been taken to make

The most northerly bus shelter on mainland Britain is near Dunnet Head, and is made from slabs of cement and aggregate, with high walls for storm protection.

One of London Transport's once numerous tubular steel shelters, offering protection from above, if little more. At Farnham Common, and still used by London Country route 441.

them blend with their surroundings. When a new one was erected beside the A6121 at Carlby for passengers using the Delaine's Bourne to Stamford route, it was built of Barnack stone, like most of the rest of that village. Again at Binstead Hill on the Isle of Wight a recent addition on Southern Vectis route 1A is in local Quarr stone, roofed (rather incongrously) with corrugated polythene sheeting.

There are a few shelters which cater for cyclists, like the one on Lincolnshire's 'Fenlander' route 507 by Old Leake Church, which has cycle racks at its rear.

Who pays for them and who is responsible for their upkeep? The answers are legion. Scattered about Britain are shelters paid for in memory of a local resident or as a souvenir of a national occasion – the Festival of Britain (1951) or the Silver Jubilee (1977), for example. On the 23 miles of the Horncastle Bus Club route across the Wolds into Louth there are shelters built by Parish Councils and by a former, defunct operator, Wrights of Louth. When somebody asked the Club's Committee who was responsible for keeping them tidy, however, that was another question!

However, there have been occasions when local residents have come to the rescue, as happened in Bridlington with the modern shelter at the junction of Sewerby Road and *Jubilee* Avenue along East Yorkshire Motor Services route 86 (now Town Bus 3/3A) in May 1977. They not only decorated the shelter in patriotic red, white and blue streamers but placed similarly coloured plants on its roof!

Some shelters have not been purpose-built, but have been adapted from earlier uses. Until the building of the town's bus station the people of Bourne, Lincs. used the ground floor of the Georgian Town Hall whilst awaiting their buses to Grantham, Sleaford and Spalding. In South Humberside there is a very fine one at the village of Redbourn, which used to be the village smithy. Since it was part of the estate of the Duke of St. Albans it bears his crest of a rampant horse on its pillared roof.

Whether they are new and shining, like the pleasing ones by St. Enoch Square in Glasgow, which I saw in 1980, or relics of a long past era; whether they are still in regular use, or like the circular, thatched one in the centre of Swarby (near Sleaford, Lincs.) no longer on any bus route, they deserve fuller study by not only the vernacular architect and the industrial archaeologist, but by the transport enthusiast as well.

Originally a tram shelter, this one in Dyke Road, Brighton has survived many near misses from passing traffic.

City Standards

What kind of buses were Glasgow, London, Leeds and Manchester buying in 1951, 1961, 1971 and 1981? STEWART BROWN provides the answers.

Above: Glasgow 1951 – an AEC Regent III with Weymann 56-seat body.

Glasgow 1951

The most popular purchase by Glasgow Corporation in the early postwar years was the AEC Regent III. Between 1948 and 1951 a total of 265 were bought and most had Metro-Cammell or Weymann bodywork. Additions to the Glasgow fleet at this time were many and varied – Daimlers and locally-built Albions; trolleybuses (the system was inaugurated in 1949); and even tramcars. Glasgow still had more trams than buses in 1951.

Bodywork came from an incredible variety of suppliers. In addition to Weymann and Metro-Cammell there were bodies from Crossley, Northern Coach Builders, Croft (a Glasgow car dealer), Scottish Commercial (the Crossley agent in Glasgow), Brockhouse (which was associated with Park Royal), Roberts (of Wakefield), Scottish Aviation (of Prestwick), Alexander (then based in Stirling and catering mainly for the SMT group) and even one double-decker from Mann Egerton. Some of these were fitted to reconditioned prewar chassis.

Glasgow's motorbus livery at this time was orange lower panels, green between decks, and cream.

London 1951

The RT needs no introduction. Production of London Transport's standard double-decker was in full swing in 1951. The RT had been conceived as early as 1937 and the last examples were built in 1954. In 1951 both the AEC and Leyland versions, RT and RTL, were being delivered. Bodywork at this time was being supplied by Park Royal, Weymann, Metro-Cammell (on RTLs), and, to a lesser degree, Saunders – all to LT's standard four-bay design.

Single-deckers played a comparatively small part in LT's operations at this time and the first of the underfloor-engined RF-class AEC Regal IVs were entering service in 1951. These had Metro-Cammell bodies and included the 25 private hire coaches with glazed cove panels. Like the RTs, the RFs were 7ft 6in wide, although 8ft wide RTW-class Leylands had been introduced to the streets of London in 1949.

Trolleybuses still had a part to play and the last 50 – three-axle BUTs of generally prewar appearance – were delivered in 1952.

London 1951 – the inevitable RT.

Leeds 1951

By 1951 the standard bus in the Leeds City Transport fleet was the Roe-bodied AEC Regent III. Between 1947 and 1952 Leeds added 180 Regents, mostly Roe-bodied, to its fleet, along with 60 Leylands, 20 Crossleys and 10 Daimlers. The Leylands and Crossleys were bought as complete vehicles with bodywork by their respective chassis builders.

Charles H. Roe Ltd, with a factory in the Crossgates district of Leeds, was an obvious choice to supply bodywork to the local municipality and had been doing so since 1925. Leeds was the first operator outside London to standardise on four-bay construction for a 26ft long double-decker and it also specified unusually deep side windows. The polished bonnet cover was another Leeds peculiarity.

The Leeds livery was changing at this time from an unusual two-tone blue to two-tone green. Exposed radiators remained in favour at Leeds during the 1950s, principally because the absence of a built-up bonnet improved engine accessibility.

Manchester 1951

The last of the famous Manchester streamlined buses entered service in 1951. There were 65 of them – Metro-Cammell-bodied Leyland Titan PD2s – the end of a line which had started in 1936 and had influenced Crossley's standard postwar body. Crossley had of course been closely involved in the original streamlined body development. The postwar Manchester streamlined body was but a shadow of its prewar counterpart. However it was still undeniably distinctive.

Crossley, Daimler and Leyland had all supplied buses to Manchester in the late 1940s; Crossley also supplied trolleybuses, the last of which entered service in 1951. These were Manchester's last Crossleys and ended a 21 year relationship, although Manchester's last trolleybuses – 62 BUTs delivered in 1955/6 – were built at the Crossley factory in Stockport which was still owned by Associated Commercial Vehicles.

Manchester's livery in 1951 was red with a cream band between decks and cream upper deck window surrounds. Buses which were 7ft 6in wide had grey roofs; 8ft wide buses had red roofs.

Leeds 1951 – AEC Regent III/Roe.

Manchester 1951 – Leyland Titan PD2/3/MCW.

Glasgow 1961

Glasgow led the move towards large forward-entrance buses by ordering 89 AEC Regent Vs and 140 Leyland Titan PD3s. All were 30ft long and had 72-seat Alexander bodywork – or Glasgow Corporation bodywork to Alexander design. Most were delivered in 1961, along with the last few traditional rear-entrance 61-seaters. All wore Glasgow's new livery of yellow and green separated by a narrow cream band: this had been introduced in 1960 to facilitate spray-painting.

However, the forward-entrance front-engined bus enjoyed brief popularity in Glasgow. When the last were being delivered in 1962 they were being hotly pursued by the first of 150 rear-engined Leyland Atlanteans. As a gesture to local feeling the PD3s and the Atlanteans had Albion badges. These large capacity buses were used in the final stages of the city's tramway replacement programme. The last tram ran in 1962.

Since 1957 Alexander had supplied all of Glasgow's double-deck motorbus bodies, apart from those built to Alexander design in the Corporation's workshops.

Glasgow 1961 – Leyland PD3/2 / Alexander.

London 1961

After the RT came the Routemaster, the ultimate in half-cab rear-entrance bus design. The Routemaster was an integral design based on AEC sub-frames and using Park Royal bodywork. Prototypes had been built by Eastern Coach Works and Weymann, both with Leyland running units, but in the end the Routemaster was an AEC-Park Royal product, although almost 500 Leyland-engined RMs were built in the mid-1960s.

By the end of 1961 around 1,000 were in service and they were being used to replace trolleybuses, the last of which was withdrawn in 1962.

The standard RM in 1961 was a 27ft 6in-long 64-seater, but in that year a batch of 24 experimental 30ft-long 72-seaters was introduced and this type later superseded the short model. Coach variants appeared in the following year for use on LT's Green Line services. Whereas Glasgow, Leeds and Manchester's 1961 deliveries have long since vanished, the Routemaster soldiers on – and looks set to do so for another decade.

London 1961 – AEC/Park Royal Routemaster.

Leeds 1961 – AEC Regent V/MCW

Leeds 1961

At the turn of the decade Leeds had three chassis and two body suppliers. AEC was supplying Regent Vs, and did so until 1966. Daimlers were also being delivered; five of the 1962 intake introduced forward-entrance buses to the fleet. The third chassis supplier was Leyland, and Leeds built up a fleet of 91 PD3s between 1958 and 1963.

Most of the bodywork was by Roe but a small number of Orion bodies were delivered from the MCW group.

Although slow to adopt front antrances and rear engines, Leeds had been quick to make the driver's job easier by adopting two-pedal control as standard. All double-deckers delivered in the decade up to 1961 were of this type.

The Leeds livery – a rather dark green – had been improved at this time by the addition of light green lower deck window surrounds – the relief had previously been a light green band between decks. The fleet name in this photograph is of a style introduced in the late 1960s.

Manchester 1961 – Leyland Titan PD2/37 / MCW.

Manchester 1961

Conservatism ruled in Manchester in 1961 with the delivery of Metro-Cammell rear-entrance bodies on Daimler CVG6 and exposed-radiator Leyland Titan PD2 chassis. The Titans even had manual gearboxes. A batch of ten Leyland Atlanteans had been delivered in 1960 and 20 Daimler Fleetlines followed in 1962 – but it was not until 1964 that the last Titans were delivered and Manchester went whole-heartedly for rear-engined buses.

A few one-man operated single-deck buses were also being bought in 1961/2, including some in an attractive blue livery.

During the late 1950s Manchester had supported both Daimler and Leyland, although not always equally – only Daimlers in 1954/5, mainly Leylands in 1956, only Daimlers in 1957, only Leylands in 1958/9. The last trolleybuses had been purchased in 1956; the system was to close in 1966.

The livery had been simplified in 1958 when spray-painting was introduced and was now all-over red with a single cream relief band.

Glasgow 1971

Atlanteans rule, OK! is a reasonable summary of the position in Glasgow in 1971. In 1958 Glasgow had been one of the first operators to place an Atlantean in service. By late 1971 it had over 550 on the road, equal to half the fleet strength.

All had Alexander bodies. The first was of the box-like appearance typical of all early rear-engined double-deckers. But the later vehicles, delivered from 1962 onwards, had very attractive bodies with curved windscreens. All but the first one were delivered in the simplified post-1960 yellow and green livery. At first 78-seat single-doorway bodies were standard but in 1969 a change was made to the then-fashionable two-door layout.

During the 1970s the body style changed with the introduction of alloy construction at Alexander, and, after the formation of the Greater Glasgow PTE in 1973, panoramic windows were adopted for a number of years. Glasgow was the biggest Atlantean operator in the world.

Glasgow 1971 – Leyland Atlantean PDR1A/1 / Alexander.

London 1971

The RT in 1951 and the RM in 1961 were both classic designs. Who would say the same of1971's double-decker – the much abused, unloved, and often unfairly criticised DMS? The DMS was a Daimler Fleetline and the first of 2,646 entered service in January 1971. The two-door body, by Metro-Cammell or Park Royal, was not inherently unattractive . . . but London Transport's unrelieved red livery did not flatter it.

While DMS delivery was just beginning, large scale delivery of single-deckers was just ending. LT's great Bus Reshaping Plan of 1966 (which did not do what the title said; buses were *not* reshaped, routes *were*) had foreseen a great future for the single-decker. Accordingly some 1,500 rear-engined AECs were purchased – and resold within ten years. The great Bus Reshaping Plan did itself need to be reshaped.

The Fleetlines were not a great success either. They were not easily adaptable to LT's maintenance system. And LT's maintenance system was apparently not easily adaptable to the Fleetline.

London 1971 – Daimler Fleetline CRG6/Park Royal.

Leeds 1971

Leeds leads, it is said – though I've yet to hear it said anywhere outside Leeds. Be that as it may, Leeds was among the leaders in bus design in 1971. A new generation of 33ft long dual-doorway double-deck buses had hit the streets of the city in 1968. They had Roe bodies – of course – and panoramic windows.

With them had come an attractive new livery layout with larger areas of light green. Leeds was still dual-sourcing its chassis and the new vehicles were of both Daimler and Leyland manufacture. Leeds was not immune to the enthusiasm sweeping the country for single-deck city buses and received its last batch of AEC Swifts in 1971. These brought to 140 the total number of rear-engined single-deckers owned. But the big double-decker was the Leeds bus of the time – there were 315 by the time the last were delivered to Leeds' successors, the West Yorkshire Passenger Transport Executive, in 1974.

Leeds 1971 – Leyland Atlantean PDR2/1 / Roe.

Manchester 1971 – Daimler Fleetline CRG6LXB-33/Park Royal.

Manchester 1971

The use of the name Mancunian for a new design of bus was a fine reflection of justifiable civic pride in Manchester. The Mancunian was a landmark in bus body design with its long deep windows and enormous windscreens. It could have looked over-square with its almost vertical sides, but a carefully thought-out red and white livery avoided that difficulty. One could wax poetic about Mancunians in Piccadilly – huge square-rigged ships cutting purposefully through the storm of peak hour traffic.

The Mancunians were based on Atlantean and Fleetline chassis and had bodies by Park Royal, East Lancs, Metro-Cammell and Roe – all to the same basic design and usually with two doors. The first vehicles were 9.5m long; the later ones were 10m. The Mancunian was designed as a one-man operated double-decker and the first vehicles had a capacity of 96 passengers of whom 73 were seated. By 1971 Manchester City Transport had given way to the Selnec PTE whose orange and white livery graced the last new Mancunians.

Glasgow 1981

Although good Glaswegians still talked about Corporation buses, by 1981 they were the property of the Strathclyde Passenger Transport Executive. Atlanteans still ruled in 1981, the year in which the last were delivered. The livery had changed twice in the decade – to green lower panels, yellow between decks and white elsewhere on the formation of the Greater Glasgow PTE in 1973, and to green lower panels, black lower deck window surrounds and a yellow top for new buses in 1981. Repaints received a variation of this livery.

Alexander bodies still predominated too, but there were signs that the old order was changing. Ailsas, Metropolitans and Metrobuses had all been bought in small numbers in the 1970s, principally to try each type out. New Ailsas were delivered in 1981, with Alexander's new R-type body.

Glasgow had been quick to try the new Atlantean in 1958 and was quick to try the new Olympian in 1981 – with bodies by Alexander, Roe and ECW. Variety rules, OK!

Glasgow 1981 – Leyland Olympian ONTL11/1R / Roe.

London 1981 – Leyland Titan TNLXB2RRSp/Park Royal.

London 1981

'Clash of the Titans' was a film on general release in London in 1981. If it had nothing else to commend it, the title seemed wryly apt as Leyland and MCW battled for London's bus business. Leyland had the Titans on its side; MCW, the Metrobi. Both were integral designs – although it would seem that some integrals were more integral than others since MCW also produced a Metrobus chassis.

In operation the Titans did not get much opportunity to Clash. The Metrobi operated in the west; the Titans in the east – and rarely the twain did meet. All were of two-door layout, a style abandoned by most operators in the mid-1970s, but still appropriate for certain types of high density urban operation.

Early deliveries were in an improved livery with white upper deck window surrounds – first seen on the last DMSs – but this was abandoned during 1979 in favour of unrelieved red. Single-deckers were still featuring in LT's buying programme too – integral Leyland National 2s.

Leeds 1981 – Leyland Atlantean AN68/1R / Roe.

Leeds 1981

The West Yorkshire Passenger Transport Executive had in 1974 combined the bus operations in the towns of Bradford, Halifax, Huddersfield and Leeds. A variety of new liveries were mooted, some were tried and abandoned, and finally a combination of verona green and cream was selected with the fleetname MetroBus – which appears somewhat inappropriate on the standard Roe-bodied Atlanteans and Fleetlines. There are some MetroBus Metrobuses, but most new double-deckers at the start of this decade were Atlanteans.

The appearance of Roe-bodied Olympians late in 1981 may presage future buying policy – and the end of the standard style of Roe body which had served the PTE since its inception. This had one door, 76 seats, and was 9.5m long. The Olympians had a new standard design of body derived from Leyland's experience with the Titan, and of a generally more modern appearance. The elimination of the prominent engine pod of the first generation of rear-engined buses was a noticeable visual improvement on the Olympian.

Manchester 1981 – Leyland Atlantean AN68/1R / Northern Counties.

Manchester 1981

After Manchester City Transport and the Mancunian came the Selnec PTE and the Selnec standard, followed by Greater Manchester Transport and the GMT standard. The Selnec and GMT standards were basically the same vehicle, a neat four-bay design which had evolved over the years and was built mainly by Northern Counties and Park Royal on Daimler Fleetline and Leyland Atlantean chassis. The closure of Park Royal and the cessation of Fleetline production put the emphasis on Northern Counties-bodied Atlanteans in 1981.

GMT was also building up a sizeable fleet of Metrobi in 1981 and, keeping its options open, had examples of Ailsa, Dennis, Leyland Olympian and Leyland Titan on the road. Oh, yes – and Foden. Two of the ill-starred Foden NCs were purchased before receivership parted Foden from the bus business.

Livery changes were also in train in Manchester. At the end of 1980 the familiar Selnec-designed orange and white was being slowly superseded by a new and attractive brown, orange and white. It became standard in 1981.

Holiday Harvest

Photographs taken on holiday by G. H. F. ATKINS

A rare 1920s model, the Vulcan 'Manchester', seen at Skegness in July 1929 in the fleet of Tom Cary Ltd, of Skegness, and used on service between North Shore and Seacroft. Livery was light grey with a white roof.

July 1929 in Skegness again, and a 'Restaurant Coach 'operated by J. Mitchell, of Derby. It was a 1930 Leyland Tiger with body by United, Lowestoft.

Continental chassis are nothing new in Britain. This Renault S1 model, owned by Bateman & Fines of Bulwell, Nottingham, was seen at Skegness in July 1929.

An Albion PM28 with 32-seat Northern Counties body, new in 1927, seen at Skegness in 1929 in the fleet of Leicester & District Green Bus Co. Ltd, who were absorbed by Midland Red in 1936, although this bus was not used.

Little remembered today, the W&G Du Cros chassis was fairly familiar at one time. This later 1920s model, seen at Skegness in 1930, was owned by T. A. Smith (Delaine), of Bourne.

Also in Skegness in 1930, one of United's once-large fleet of ADC 425s. This bus, with United 35-seat two-door body, was new in 1928. Note the little Chevrolet bringing up the rear.

This smart Crosville Leyland Tiger TS3 was seen at Llandudno in June 1933, carrying a 25-seat Leyland rear-entrance body. It was rebodied by ECW in 1939.

In picturesque Lee Bay, Devon, in June 1932, a Western National AEC Reliance with Strachan body on the service to Ilfracombe.

A wet day in Torquay in May 1937, and a Devon General petrol-engined Leyland Lion LT5 with Brush 31-seat body. One of three bought in 1934, it was pressed into military service in 1940.

In Lyme Regis in May 1937, a smart Devon General Harrington-bodied Leyland Tiger TS7 petrol. New in 1936, it went to the War Department in 1940, and later went to Ribble, where it received a Burlingham body and 7.4 litre oil engine.

Girls chewing things, with an impressive line of buses behind shining in the evening sun.

Birmingham Sessions, Impressions and Digressions

ROBERT E. JOWITT

There is a notable poem by Sebastian Evans (1830-1909) relating how the Abbot of Saint Werewulf Juxta Slingsby, after complicated dealings with a poached pike, acquires a rare manuscript; this poem, of some 500 lines, is, says George McBeth, editor of the *Penguin Book of Victorian Verse,* a splendid example of development by digression. And I feel, after considering the matter throughout a sleepless night, that I can best describe my relationship with the great city of Birmingham in similar vein, in progression by a series of digressions, though not, I hasten to add, in verse.

That whole paragraph is a digression. . .

So far as I recall, my first visit to Birmingham is in the mid 1960s. I am being helpful by taking some chairs from my grandmother to her niece who must be my cousin-once-removed and this cousin lives about 15 miles from Birmingham, but she is away from home when I deliver the chairs so I can't stay in her mansion but have to stay – admittedly at her expense – at an adjacent smart hotel where nevertheless I am greeted by a youth with a shotgun who says they aren't serving dinner and I must eat elsewhere. Anyway, as I am near Birmingham, I think it a good opportunity to look at the Burne-Jones stained glass angels in Birmingham Cathedral, and also the Town Hall with which I am long familiar through having a picture of it on the cover of – unlikely though it may seem – a Chris Barber record. And while I am about it, I also take a few photos of the buses, nice half-cab blue-and-cream double deckers, for although while I am in the Black Country I am hastening as soon as I have my fill of Burne-Jones to Walsall and Wolverhampton to see the trolleybuses which must surely be much more meritorious than any motor buses I do realise, by instinct and the pages of *Buses Illustrated* and by my own observations on the spot, that these buses are unique to Birmingham and I doubt there can be any others like them, and I am subsequently glad that I take these pictures for they prove to be the only pictures I have showing these buses with their Birmingham aura; and one of them is reproduced on p74 of *Buses Annual 1979.*

Edward Burne-Jones, celebrated Victorian painter and native of Birmingham, would surely have found the features of this flowerily-bloused maiden entirely in the classic Pre-Raphaelite mould.

So the next time I am in Birmingham is in 1972 and in rather different circumstances, for I am driving my own bus – which happens to be a 1936 Renault from Paris – in the Lord Mayor's Procession, carrying advertisements to celebrate the *n*th anniversary of BEA flights from Brum to Paree, which advertisements are obviously quite suitable on my bus; and thus I am housed in great luxury by courtesy of BEA in the Airport hotel while my bus is housed in a nearby hangar which probably for my bus also represents quite a degree of luxury, but Birmingham Airport bears scant relation to Birmingham itself and when I am actually in Birmingham I am far too occupied driving my own bus to think about the native buses. This event being now a long time ago, I recall very little about it save that while I am parked behind the Police Station, which has no bearing on any misdemeanour of mine because of course I do not commit misdemeanours but it happens to be the place where part of the Lord Mayor's Procession starts. . . while, as I repeat after that digression, I am parked there, a curious figure approaches the bus. Now I tell this story many times afterwards, and possibly it grows in the telling, and therefore possibly I do the curious figure an injustice, but in my mind the figure is clad in a sinister macintosh and is of shuffling gait. Anyway, he says to me: "Scuse me asking, but is this bus French?" and "Scuse me asking, but how old is this bus?" and "Scuse me asking, etc. etc." There is in truth nothing very remarkable about people asking questions in this vein, as I learn over the years, for even when I have pos and neg wires rubbing together and the whole of the inside of the bus is filled with smoke and I am frantically isolating everything in reach there is still some tomfool standing at the back asking inane questions, but I do here mention this questioner in Birmingham as he is the subject of another digression which those readers who can bear to persevere with this history can see in a moment.

Meanwhile, I am again in Birmingham in January 1973, again driving my 1936 Renault, this time to celebrate the opening of a new hotel, so of course again I can pay very little attention to the indigenous buses, though I do seem to recall that some of the old ones are still around, though perhaps now described as West Midlands rather than sporting fine Birmingham coats-of-arms, and I also observe some single-deck Fleetlines which strike me as rather splendid in a freakish sort of way. So far as the hotel is concerned, on one of the first nights that it is open a diner complains that the pâté is off and walks out. I mean to say by this that the diner walks out, but if what the diner says about the pâté is true it might very well be the pâté which is walking out. I hear subsequently that the hotel and the chain to which it belongs go bust, and this of course may be because of the pâté. I cannot think that it is in any way my fault, for I am sure that the presence of an antique Paris bus is a very good way to publicise the opening of a new hotel, and I hope anyone thinking of branching out in the hotel line contacts me without delay.

But before this hotel chain goes bust, it opens another hotel in Leicester, and so I go to Leicester in my 1936 Renault to celebrate this event too, and by now it is May, and in the evenings after I park my bus in the Corporation bus garage I am able to photograph the buses of Leicester, and as some of them are AEC double-deckers and some of them are Metro-Scania single-deckers they remind me very much, though they are in different livery, of the King Alfred buses in my own city of Winchester. So far as the hotel is concerned, there are no complaints about the pâté. . . or not so far as I ever discover. What I do discover is a very beautiful girl who works on the hotel switchboard, and she is not unlike a Burne-Jones angel, so I drive her round Leicester in the cab of my 1936 Renault, because she thinks my bus is very beautiful, and I drive her to her home in Wigston Fields which is a suburb of Leicester and we finish off a bottle of liquor which the hotel VIPs kindly leave or inadvertently forget in my bus and I meet her Mum and her Dad and her dog and I am greatly attracted by her and if it were *Woman's Own* fiction it might be said that I am 'in love' with her; and perhaps to some extent this is reciprocated but I have to

Girls looking to see if there are any more Fleetlines coming.

take my bus away because it is going on the Brighton Run in a couple of days, so all the way down through Northampton and Newport Pagnell I sing 'Irene Goodnight' to myself (or in fact I sing this girl's name, which rhymes with 'Irene') and I drive the bus through puddles to see in the mirror the steam coming off the tail pipe – which sport for some reason suits my sad frame of mind – and eventually the silencer drops off but this is probably because it is rotten after many years service in Paris rather than because I drive through puddles. Anyway, though I no longer now remember, I expect that I send the girl some prints of the photos I take of her standing by my bus – and these are the only pictures of Leicester that I ever bother to print, the rest just remain negatives doubtless acquiring great historic value and possibly to appear in *Buses Annual 1999* if I and it still survive at that date – and apart from that I have unfortunately no further dealings with this maiden. So now a thousand years later I add this major digression on Leicester to the words about Birmingham mainly because it seems to be expected of me that I write of romantic episodes, to leaven, as it may be said, the bus loaf, in the pages of *Buses Annual;* and also in the faint hope that, should the girl see these pages, she can know that I still remember her.

Returning to Birmingham, this time a few months later, I am on my way to the Grand Transport Extravaganza, and this time I come into Birmingham in my new bus, my 1933 Renault, and this time I am in Birmingham for perhaps 10 minutes or so, parked most improperly on a double yellow line on a roundabout, to alert the Birmingham evening paper about the fact that the Extravaganza is shortly commencing and that all good citizens of Birmingham should not fail to attend. And while I am parked thus waiting on the convenience of the camera-men, a figure in a sinister macintosh shuffles up to the bus and says ''Scuse me asking, but is this bus a different bus than the one etc, etc, etc . .''

Follows a lapse of some years, and now in 1979 I am travelling by train from Chester to Winchester (and this is quite an impressive-sounding ticket to ask for at the booking-office) but I have my dear dog with me (such a fine dog that he is portrayed on pages 31 and 35 of *Buses Annual 1977*) and this dog does not like being kept in a train for several hours, so I have to plan my journey with plenty of what are described in the USA as 'Comfort Stops,' the first in Crewe, the second in Birmingham, and so on. . . Thus I arrive at New Street Station, and walk with eager dog through part of the Bull Ring to the church

Oblivious to tulips, to five buses in a row, and to whatever that man is doing with his hat.

Right: Front view of rear-engined single-deck Fleetline with Marshall body.

with a spire. I do not exactly at this moment remember just which Saint this church is dedicated to or called after, but such of my readers as know Birmingham must know which church I mean, and such as don't know are not likely to care. And by this church I sit down on a little wall, and start to eat the sandwiches which my dear mother is kind enough to provide for me. And while I – and my dog – are eating these sandwiches there is a constant and magnificent string of buses passing. None, now, certainly, of the half-cabs of days of yore, but nevertheless an endless brigade of buses in a more-or-less Birmingham blue-and-cream and certainly exuding a thoroughly Birmingham or should-I-say West Midlands atmosphere, and all the time I am watching with one eye these buses and with the other eye my sandwiches disappearing into my dog (not in fact that I am cross-eyed; I am speaking figuratively,) I am wishing that I can be taking photos of these buses. But I know very well that if I attempt to photograph them the dog must engage in his favourite habit of pulling on the end of his leash and ruining every picture by shaking the camera. So I give up thinking about taking photographs and instead I take the dog for a walk until it is time for the next train; and I do not here think fit to digress further about this journey, merely reassuring my readers that eventually I arrive safely at Winchester where, it may be recalled, I am aiming to arrive; without, however, any new photographs of Birmingham buses.

So a year later I am making the same journey again from Chester to Winchester, and if my readers wonder how I manage to be doing this or in other words how I return from Winchester to Chester I have to reply that the northward journey avoids Birmingham and has therefore no place in these pages. Now this time my journey is not encumbered by the dog, for the dog is waiting for my return, sitting in Winchester with tail ready to wag in ardent greeting, or so I imagine. But as I am dogless, I do think I have an excellent chance to do something about Birmingham, including staying the night there at the house of a famous person whose attic I am privileged to share with a number of very beautiful models of Birmingham tramcars. So all arrangements are made, and I think I have photographs of Birmingham buses at last virtually in my pocket, but it so happens that the day which I elect to travel from Chester to Birmingham is the 'Day of Action' which as many people make haste to point out is a

101
CENTREBUS
BON 468C

Rear view of single-deck Fleetline.

complete misnomer because the general idea of the Day is that there is no Action, no normal activity. And part of this non-action is that there are no trains from Chester to Crewe, but as the whole thing is a farce there are perfectly adequate trains from Chester to Shrewsbury and from Shrewsbury to Wolverhampton and even from Wolverhampton to Birmingham, so the result for me is that I have a pleasant railway journey over routes I might never otherwise encounter and an hour in Shrewsbury to sample pubs and second-hand book shops – not really quite long enough – and an hour in Wolverhampton to meditate on the futility of days of action. It is only when I arrive in Birmingham itself that the obnoxiousness of the Day of Action really inconveniences me; it transpires that a major percentage of the Birmingham buses are victims of this action, and thus inactive, so my visions of photographing hundreds of buses in the brilliant early summer evening rush hour remain mere visions. But I have to count my blessings and catch one of the small percentage of non-active buses, which, being non-active, is running, to travel to that happy house with the model trams in the attic. I must here add that as well as trams in the attic there is a real 1929 Dennis bus in the road outside, and the next morning I am driven in this Dennis via several little known but excellent architectural delights of Birmingham to New Street, so that even if this day is another Day of Action I am not deprived of transport. But it so happens that this is a day of – well, presumably, inaction. . . so all the buses are running as normal.

So I spend the next eight hours walking round and round in a small area contained on the north by Colmore Row and the west by the Town Hall and the south by New Street Station and the east by Bull Street and High Street. And apart from a couple of very necessary visits into pubs at lunchtime I am continually photographing the buses.

Only not just the buses.

I must here explain that I like my photographs of buses to be ornamented with girls (See *Buses Annual 1974*, pages 112-117). Now as must be apparent I am not in Birmingham in the late 1960s which is the golden era of girls in miniskirts and the best possible time to take photographs of girls and buses; in fact the best miniskirt photographs I have are of tramcars in Zurich and trolleybuses in Marseilles, but this is a digression. But now in 1980, even if we are in an era when a lot of girls wear incredibly ugly baggy pants and other awful garments and seem to believe – quite erroneously – that there is something alluring about the attire of para-troopers or boilermen or Mid-west hicks, nevertheless by way of compensation certain girls of this era wear incredibly tight jeans which in many ways are as meritorious as miniskirts. Tight jeans do a lot to improve the landscape which the rather dismal West Midlands buses by themselves might not make very marvellous

It is at this point, while I am pursuing the hinder quarters of Atlanteans and second-hand DMSs and tightly stretched denim along New Street and Corporation Street, that my very ageing 2¼ square Yashica starts to show its age. I have to wind on by guess rather than automatically. How many of these beautiful backsides am I shooting on backing paper or empty spool? So I buy another five rolls in Boots, and then not very long after another five rolls in a camera shop for more than a pound less – someone is slipping somewhere – and I am constantly putting in a new roll and constantly putting a Castella in my mouth and lighting it from the end of the last one because of the suspense and praying that I have the new film in and that the particular photogenic maiden I am chasing at the moment doesn't disappear into one of the all too many fashion shops before a bus sets itself in a photogenic position behind her.

And then as the afternoon wears on and I am nearly dead with continuous walking round these few brief but endless hundred yards of streets something starts happening and there begin to be more and more buses and the sun is sinking lower and casting a sort of long light down the streets; and despite the awful mess of motor car traffic and despite the fact that the sun now either makes the girls screw their faces into dreadful contortions or else leaves their faces in total darkness, and despite the fact that nearly all the buses are fairly ordinary and possibily even nasty sorts of buses, these buses come through this

Digression from Birmingham: the golden age of miniskirts – 1969 – with an equally attractive background of Zurich tramways.

declining sunlight in sufficient quantity and with sufficient presence that they assume an aura or a glamour or some sort of air which, spurious though it probably is, smacks heavily of vanished and unreclaimable evenings in Glasgow with trams screaming past in droves, or of evenings which if not vanished or unreclaimable yet are difficult to obtain because they are so far away because they are in Lisbon. . . but just at this moment this mass of buses in Birmingham, strings of them with the sun shining behind them and highlighting their filthy clouds of exhaust, conjures up the whole beauty of public service vehicles which normally are mundane but which can sometimes as now be marvellous beyond compare. . .

So I go on taking photos until the light is threatening to wither and destroy the magic it is making up till now, and until the camera is becoming almost unmanageable, and until I miss the last but one reasonable train to Winchester. Then I go to New Street, and I buy a bottle of wine in the station concourse, and in a happy haze of fatigue and Beaujolais I watch the evening countryside of Warwickshire and Oxfordshire speed past the carriage window, and I don't care very much if half the photos of the backs of Birmingham buses and Birmingham girls don't come out.

By now, I have forgotten already most of what I have taken, but I know that I have tried, and that I have lived a splendid day. The click of the shutter time and time again, the thrill of the hunt, this was enough. If the photos come out, so much the better. Another pull of red wine. Soon I'll be back with my dog.

The famous London-based private bus and coach operator, Birch Brothers Ltd., operated a varied and interesting fleet. The stage carriage services in the Bedford and Hitchin areas, and the famous 203 service from London to Rushden, were acquired by United Counties in 1968/69. This 1947 Leyland Titan PD1 was originally fitted with lowheight forward-entrance Birch body, but is seen in Hitchin in 1966 carrying the 56-seat Metro-Cammell Orion body it received in 1957. It was withdrawn in 1967.

Below: In 1950 Birch received five of these Leyland Comet CPO1 with 32-seat coach bodies by Windover, and one is seen at Luton railway station early in 1962, shortly before withdrawal.

Bring Back Birch?

Photographs by G. R. MILLS

This 1954 AEC Reliance 470, seen in Luton in 1964, carries an ECW-like Park Royal Royalist 41-seat coach body. It was sold in 1966.

Another AEC Reliance 470 with Park Royal body, one of two 45-seat buses delivered in 1958. It is seen in Bedford in 1963.

One of six rare Commer-Beadle TS3s supplied to Birch in 1955, seen at Newmarket on a race day in 1962. It was withdrawn in 1964.

There were three of these 1959 Leyland Tiger Cub PSUC1/2 with 41-seat Willowbrook coach bodies. One is seen at Bedford in 1966.

Birch received three of these Leyland Leopards with 51-seat Willowbrook bodies in 1962 – early examples of the now familiar 36ft long single-decker.

A later Birch Leopard, one of four 1965 PSU3/3R with Marshall 49-seat bodywork, seen on route 203 in Hitchin in 1966.

Signs of the Times

JOHN E. DUNABIN

Timetable fascination must have ensnared me long before I could recognize myself as a bus enthusiast. Our local service, 'Suburban', produced a plain card folder, which really told me what all the village knew, buses to town every 40 minutes in the mornings, doubled to every 20 minutes in afternoons, evenings, and all day on Saturdays, but for me it was absorbing reading.

Additionally, although my parents were very keen motor cyclists, and rarely travelled by public transport apart from infrequent shopping trips to Liverpool, there was usually a current Crosville timetable in the house. I derived pleasure from the outline illustration of a bus on the cover, and can remember from long ago the mild excitement when the new edition sported a PLSC – known merely as a 'Lion' in those days – in place of the high built SG. The appearance of extra lines on the map over the years, as the book's thickness gradually increased, was something else to enjoy.

These were not quite the only sources of bus information available close at hand. Inside the kitchen cupboard hung one of those sheets the size of a newspaper (non-tabloid), commonly used to publicize things like football fixtures, and paid for by the advertisers whose displays formed a border to the essential information. This one was designed, inter alia – or perhaps it was just another advertisement, memory is not clear on the point – to disseminate information on times of the joint service of Lancashire United and St Helens Corporation between Warrington and St Helens.

But I must keep my sights on what I set out to write about, public, not private, displays. So far as I was aware there always were wall timetables, even though not all operators made much if any use of them. We in my village were lucky in that Crosville did so, and in generous fashion. Mr Pusill, owner of 'Suburban', followed suit later and to a limited extent; perhaps

Below: Southgate Street coach station, Leicester, in 1959 with Midland Red LD8 and D7 buses plus numerous timetable cases, and a blackboard to give extra information.

he just copied big brother. Crosville wall timetables started off as large sheets of paper, headed but otherwise blank, on which were typed the times of buses passing a named point (in passing, there must have been a special wide carriage typewriter at Crane Wharf). While at town terminals the sheet may have got filled, in our village and I am sure in many other places there was much empty space. Perhaps the standard size was adopted to aid recognition, or possibly a different form of display had been intended. Other thoughts prevailed later.

Lancashire United, when I first noticed any of its publicity, was using a similar layout. The North Western Road Car Co and Ribble Motor Services however adopted a different approach, needing larger timetable frames, which contained printed timetables, all on one sheet, for all the services they operated in the area. Commonly, if not in both these two cases – memory fails me here – such sheets used the type set for the company's booklet timetables. United Automobile Services, I observed later, did not do this, but had special display timetables in much larger type (Bristol Omnibus, London Transport, and possibly others do so nowadays), and Ribble varied its approach, producing for some towns special sheets which also included a summary of departures.

This style of presentation was also used in Preston by two of the larger independents, Dallas and Fishwick, until the disappearance of the former and integration of the latter's services with those of Ribble in 1935. It certainly was not used everywhere by Ribble in the late 1920s and early 1930s. The large red-framed board, screwed to the wall of the Grosvenor Hotel, across the square from school, was part of the street furniture in the centre of Widnes. No Ribble buses were ever in view when I looked out, but by carefully sifting all the information there I learned of an hourly service on Sundays only to St Helens and Wigan.

So far I have written 'board', but all the street timetables I saw were in glass fronted cabinets, even those of the small operators I discovered during summer holidays. Widening horizons introduced me to other styles. Red & White went in for open boards, with the timetable sheet gummed to the board; Midland Red had some open boards and some glass-fronted, possibly being in process of changing over to the latter type when I first became able to observe the situation in depth. Occasionally one found that somebody had torn away part – the most studied one – of the exposed sheet, but never, until the late 1950s, did I see signs of deliberate breakage of any glass fronts. Even now, and not far from where I write, I can expect to find an intact cabinet of the type used by the same operator 50 years and more ago.

Unbroken glass helps to preserve the sheet behind, but does in some areas, following a particular cycle of temperature/humidity, trap enough condensation to make the underlying information unreadable. Of course, siting a wall timetable outside the range of streetlamps can mean that it is useless to the casual traveller after dark, unless he is equipped with torch or matches. Fortunately high winds and condensation don't go together.

A word should be added in passing about colour. It may seem pretty obvious to identify buses and services with wall timetables, but it could have been just availability of that colour of paint. Some modern liveries would prove difficult to reproduce in fibreglass, but careful matching no longer seems to be of much importance now there is virtually no competition. And think of advertising ('all over') buses.

Apart from the glass/no glass schools, there have clearly been some regional differences of size, shape, and positioning. Nowhere – or I should write hardly anywhere – else have I seen timetable frames of the size favoured by Ribble and North Western, but of course, if you put your information on the lamp post type of bus stop sign, in London Transport style, there is a severe size limit. Crosville recognised this, and departed from its own standard in favour of something much narrower when there was no wall near the bus stop. Other operators, even when walls were available, seemed to think that small was, if not beautiful, best.

Shapes varied too, longer than wide in Lancashire and Cheshire, squat in some other places. Square tops seem to have been the norm, but gable ends were much in favour in the East Midlands, and the style spread to Swansea, or did it go the other way? It was in South Wales too, actually in territory shared by three major operators and two independents at the time, where I saw my favourite timetable, two clock faces – the service ran hourly in each direction – in the operator's garage window.

This was an oddity. While many independents, and some of the major operators too, were not fully sold on the idea of this sort of publicity, observations made in the five or six years before the last war, mostly in the Welsh Border area but with forays elsewhere, showed that many, even those with perhaps only a single bus, thought it worth while to advertise along their line of route. Furthermore, those who did believed in going to the expense of having their timetables printed.

Rescued from the loft after thirty years.

On the wall of the disused Wayne Smithy, alongside his market bus route from Michaelchurch to Abergavenny, Mr Morris of Longtown had his timetable displayed, and not just a sheet of paper nailed to a door but with a proper board to back it. In much more metropolitan surroundings (at Allensmore actually) Mr E. E. Williams of Pontrilas also used a deserted smithy to advertise his service to Hereford. His successor, Mr W. E. Morgan, was apparently an unbeliever; the green board remained devoid of information.

Yeomans Motors of Canon Pyon was running many services even in 1939, and its glass fronted cabinets – this was the raeson for writing 'hardly anywhere' above – were amongst the largest I ever saw. Some of the detail, of services relatively far away, must have been of very little use to passers by, but as an indication of omnipresence it may have had its value. It was to me a cheering sight on coming into an unfamiliar village to see a timetable board, better still to see more than one, even if I had chosen a blank day for buses. This indicates another method of travel, necessary even then in places such as Central Wales, if one didn't want to camp out overnight. Cycling into the small village of Church Stoke, set in fairly empty country, it was pleasing, even reassuring, to see a row of three boards there advertising the services of three different operators.

Further surprises there were, usually in villages and not towns. Timetable boards were easy to spot, and so were other signs, such as patches of oil on roads – bus termini at a guess! Seeing a small poster on the side of a clapboard barn in Woofferton picturing a handsome looking coach made me stop sharply. From this I became aware of Owens of Abberley, and their summer express service from Kidderminster to Aberystwyth. Sadly, I didn't think to follow this up by seeking a full timetable. Many years later, in Ludlow, I saw some fascinating but incomplete information – the tearers had not done a proper job! – about other services in this area, and wrote off to the address that still remained, hoping to learn more. Nothing came; Mr Holt of Orleton had alas gone out of business years before.

This leads me to another aspect of wall timetables; one might possibly call it persistence of vision. When a bus operator withdraws from an area, by sale or otherwise, his buses sooner or later disappear, certainly his livery vanishes, but some evidence of his former presence may remain. Mr Morris of Longtown did not feel obliged to remove the 'Red & White' board nailed to a tree – his tree I feel sure – alongside his garage, when the company withdrew from that area. It remained there for perhaps ten years, a tantalising reminder of what I had missed. Others might have felt more sadness at seeing an undamaged but blank Midland Red board in Welshpool. Thirty five years after John Hirst's last bus ran through the town on service, there was still a painted board at Rhodes Bank, Oldham, showing the times of 'Ripponden District' buses to Halifax. I kept meaning to ask if I could have this memento, then alas it vanished, perhaps to make firewood.

Another relatively ancient monument, on the wall of the 'Flat Iron' building in central Manchester (the yard below, where independent buses and coaches gathered, was I believe known as Poets Corner), advertised the long vanished service of Tognarellis to Bolton. Less easy to remove, because it was painted in large white letters on stone, it reminded me nevertheless of some of the cruder forms of timetable. I never saw any of the chalk-on-road announcements used in the early days by some operators before respectability of image became important – Midland Red I believe was one! – but the noted Samuel Ledgard, or perhaps 'Exors of' by this time, relied even in postwar years on chalk and the wall – clapboard again – of a Post Office building in the centre of Leeds. The display of a printed timetable or even a handwritten one in a shop window was vastly superior to this. I first learned of Dixon's service between Doncaster and Consett from a small piece of brown cardboard in the window of a Waterdale snack bar. Setting a somewhat higher standard, the 'GNE' service to Carlisle was modestly advertised in Darlington by means of a small printed sheet in a shop window across the street from its starting point.

Such notices have only a limited life, with or without glass fronts, but timetable boards can endure, as did that of Ripponden District Motors. Up and down the country various Women's Institutes, gardening societies, cricket clubs, etc, make thair activities known, like foxes in badger setts, using emptied bus timetable cabinets. The one in Warrington which had advertised 'Suburban' times to Penketh and Sankey remained for many years to remind me of more exciting times, but the information there, of meetings, whist drives, rambles, and other relatively uninteresting activities, meant nothing. One unused for any of these purposes remained in a loft at Leintwardine until a bus enthusiast, interested not in current times but in what they had been 30 years earlier, happened to be passing.

Perhaps the most surprising use of an old board was made known to enthusiasts visiting Nottingham City Transport a few years ago. Formerly giving information about the services run by Mr Clark of Epperstone, who sold out not to NCT but to Mansfield and District, it now served, with hooks screwed into it, as a key board.

The oldest timetable I have seen on public display (excluding tattered fragments which could not easily be removed) dated back 25 years – Yorkshire economical instincts coming to the fore here – but still appeared to be correct. Only once have I found the times shown to be wrong, meaning at variance with what the operator intended to run! This left me with another two hours to wait, but as the official who should have replaced it with a revised version was an old friend, the vitriolically-worded letter to Head Office was never posted.

Timetables on display say to the potential traveller: 'We are here, and are going your way (sometimes)'. Timetable boards may say to the budding historian: 'We have been here'. They could at one time – before we all knew so much – make the bus enthusiast aware of operators and services he knew nothing of. Twenty five years ago, when travelling as passenger in a fast car through a part of the East Midlands where I thought I knew everything I wanted to know about stage operation, a roadside board flashed across my field of view with the word 'COMFORT' in large letters on it. My driver, having other interests, couldn't stop to let me confirm my suspicions, even on the return journey, but it was really quite easy to link the word with Gibson Bros. of Barlestone. Few such surprises can be left, but I am still compelled to scan every likely-looking board whenever I travel outside the fully 'Nationalised' or 'PTEd' deserts.

Not Like It Used To Be

JOHN ALDRIDGE

All too often one hears people remark that such-and-such a bus undertaking is not like it used to be. The comment certainly applies to London Country Bus Services and, strangely, is as appropriate now – in 1982 – as it was about ten years ago.

The last day of 1981 East Grinstead garage closed. And in a splendid gesture some of its last journeys were worked by an ex-London Transport Park Royal-bodied Daimler Fleetline. An Alexander-bodied AEC Swift was also operational early in December.

To both vehicles attaches quite a tale.

LCBS was set up as the result of a political decision to give control of London Transport to the Greater London Council. Strangely, too, the original decision to set up LT was also a political decision. The planners and politicians of the late 1920s and early 1930s took a broad view of the likely spread of London and its environs, which was why all bus, tram, trolley bus and tube undertakings within a fairly wide – and carefully defined – radius of central London came under the wing of LT compulsorily.

The view taken in the late 1960s had to be less altruistic because the GLC was not really likely to be interested in any network of bus services which served areas beyond its own boundaries. Buses or public transport in 1970 was not the money-making enterprise it was, in general, in 1930, though to be fair it must be remembered that LT in the mid-1930s had some difficulty in making the dividend payments on its share stock that it was supposed to, in fact was required to.

When LT went to the GLC the deal was accompanied by a write-off of almost all its capital debts. The part of LT that was hived off elsewhere was LT's country bus and coach section whose garages and whose country bus routes were in general outside the GLC area. They went to the National Bus Company, in almost debt-free form, and LCBS began trading on January 1, 1970.

But if LCBS was debt-free it was also fairly devoid of useful assets, its main (and almost only) possessions being the (ageing) vehicles and the garages they stood in at night.

It is probably not unfair to say that in the 1960s, when private car competition became more marked, LT tended to regard its green bus section as a kind of cross it had to bear. The green bus people might go for long periods with no or virtually no new vehicles, and then receive a big batch. For example, there had been 100 long Routemaster double-deck buses delivered in 1965-66 and they were the first new deckers (apart from Green Line vehicles) since the 1950s.

So NBC acquired or came into the possession of a bus company with vehicles and garages but virtually none of the supporting services – some 50 in all – that are essential to run any bus company. For these, of which a payrolls department and an overhaul works are just two examples, LCBS was still dependent on LT, only gradually building up its own facilities though anxious to do this as it probably paid a fairly high price for them as LT's style of working was more expensive.

Of the vehicles, the newest were in the single-deck fleet where there were just over 100 AEC Merlins in service, with 138 AEC Swifts on order. But LCBS saw as one of its many priorities the necessity to do something drastic about the large number (about 500) of aged 1940s and 1950s RT type double-deckers still running – all with conductors, of course. The record on the single-deck side was rather better, with most of the routes worked by RFs (dating from the early 1950s) already one-man operated.

Green Line routes were also identified as being in urgent need of new rolling stock, not because the vehicles were old but because they were not capable of being one-man worked and yet the routes were losing money. Given the benefit of hindsight, LT's decisions, implemented in 1962 and 1965, to double-deck most coach routes and at the same time to halve the frequencies was incredible. It was apparently made because LT could not get agreement for one-man operation of existing routes but at the very least the decision must have thrown away an enormous amount of traffic. Run any service through congested London suburbia and time keeping will be varied, but with half-hourly services if the would-be passenger is patient a coach is likely to turn up. Widen the headway to an hour and the effects of late running or a missed journey are horrific.

All that should explain why LCBS needed new vehicles desperately, as just one of its major problems. Because the order books of the bus industry were somewhat full, it had to take what it was offered and that included, luckily for LCBS, some new or nearly-new vehicles from one or two Welsh NBC subsidiaries which were themselves in financial difficulties at the time.

And now, if we turn back to East Grinstead garage on December 31, 1981, the Fleetline was the last operational LCBS bus then that had come from LT. Not only has the

Left: One of around 500 RTs inherited by London Country when London Transport passed to the GLC. At Staines station, it sports the original 'wheelbarrow' LCBS symbol.

Right: A surpising acquisition was a tiny fleet of ex-Southdown Leyland Tital PD3s with Northern Counties bodies. They were based at Godstone.

Most Routemasters were sold back to LT, with most of the short coaches, like RMC1494, becoming training vehicles, still in green.

Right: The Alexander-bodied AEC Swifts were popular with passengers and staff, and at least one did tours and hire work from Crawley – seen here in Redhill.

fleet therefore completely changed in those 12 years, but a considerable number of vehicles bought subsequently have also vanished.

Those first ten years could certainly be described by anyone with LCBS throughout as traumatic. Perhaps it was the effects of the three-day week (remember the miners' strike?) that helped bring the company to its lowest ebb. A friend there told me that at most garages Monday morning began with nearly enough vehicles to meet the morning peak requirement, but the position steadily deteriorated through the week to the Friday evening peak, when the most unlikely vehicles might turn up, but the most journeys would be missed.

Meanwhile there was all the week-end overtime in the world for any garage staff who wanted it, as they worked like beavers to get vehicles back on the road for Monday morning.

Supervision on the road was poor too for the volume of public complaint was so great that more and more inspectors were spending most of their time not trying to conjure up a reasonable service despite vehicle shortages, but trying to find out why X, Y, Z and all the others hadn't run last week so that letters of explanation could be written to the complainants.

Only the other day I talked to an LCBS driver of many years' service who told me he didn't really like local bus work ('get fed up with going round and round the houses') but had given up Green Line driving after a cross-London run on which he was the first vehicle for three hours. 'The aggro was so terrible that I just vowed to give it up' he told me.

To be fair LCBS did its very best to overcome the problems, and hired in whatever vehicles it could find. At one stage there were Royal Blue Bristol single-deckers working out of Dunton Green garage, Eastbourne Corporation AEC Regent Vs at Swanley, and you could find yellow Bournemouth 'deckers from Leatherhead garage meeting blue and yellow Maidstone 'deckers from Chelsham at Croydon, to name the more interesting. The hired vehicles in general were maintained by their owners and this and the quite long-term nature of some of the hiring enabled the maintenance staff to get on top of maintenance of LCBS vehicles.

But we have jumped forward in time. When LCBS came into being in 1970 its owners, NBC, were also new. They too had only just begun to sort out vehicle orders, standardisation, plans and other matters that had been dealt with in different fashions by the erstwhile Tilling and BET groups.

LCBS placed big orders for vehicles as well as picking up diverted orders from the temporarily poor sister undertakings. The big orders were for 90 AEC Reliances (because delivery was good) with, unusually, Park Royal bodies (because the bodybuilder, at that time mainly concentrating on double-deckers, had spare capacity), and for 90 Leyland Atlanteans, also with Park Royal bodies. Another 30 similar Atlanteans with Metro-Cammell bodies were a diverted Midland Red order and all 120 were a half-way model between the earlier PDR type and the later AN68. Probably LCBS would have preferred Daimler Fleetlines if they had been available, but hindsight this time shows it to have been a good choice.

The only Fleetlines to be added to the fleet were 11 intended for Western Welsh, with Northern Counties bodies and Leyland engines. They went to work at Godstone garage on route 410 in February 1972, in what was the first one-man double-deck operation of size in the company. Ironically when LT put long Routemasters on to the 409, 410 and 411 routes in the mid 1960s that was to use the larger capacity (72 seats against an RT's 56) to cut the losses on these services.

Other purchases were AEC Swifts with Marshall and Willowbrook bodies which were bought new by South Wales Transport but moved to LCBS after only a few months. More interesting were the 21 Swifts with Alexander bodies ordered by South Wales but diverted to LCBS before being built.

The story is strange. The early gestation period in NBC which I have mentioned had meant that the headquarters

TOUR
FROM
CRAWLEY
PAY AS
YOU
ENTER
PLEASE
JPF 120K

staff when sorting out the year's order programme concentrated first on the bulk requirements for such vehicles as Bristol VRTs. When they got round to smaller orders such as Swifts for ex-BET companies with AEC fleets they found most bodybuilders were fully committed. But Walter Alexander of Falkirk was persuaded to fit out a bus version of its coach body for South Wales Transport. Before they were built LCBS came along, wanted some coaches, and was able to persuade Alexander to coach fit and trim these 'buses'. In my opinion with their gently sloping flat floor they had a neater interior and far, far better visibility for passengers than any true coach design. However, the lack of luggage accommodation would not have made them attractive for extended tour or long distance work. Their relatively short length meant that the smaller engine – the AH505 8.2 litre – was fitted and this did not give a terribly sparkling performance, though they were quite popular with drivers.

Since those halcyon days, LCBS vehicle policy has been fairly logical and consistent with now a big fleet of Atlanteans and the world's biggest fleet of Leyland Nationals, including some of the very first to be built. There was a surprising purchase in the Summer of 1977 when ten secondhand former Barton Reliances were bought from a dealer. They had Plaxton coach bodies with three-and-two seating, also coach style but without headrests, and originally seated 64 but were downseated to 60 before re-entering service. They appear to be particularly useful for contract work – something LCBS has developed considerably – but can be found working as Green Lines from time to time or even occasionally instead of double-deckers.

If Green Line services were once the greatest problem area for LCBS they must surely be rated now as its greatest success. But a route map for 1982 would have little in common with one for 1970. For the whole nature and scope of the services has been changed . . . after a first few, tentative, steps. First hurdle to overcome was probably subsidies for the routes where they ran in the GLC area which virtually all did.

More important, and almost insuperable, was the loss-making nature of most and the ever-declining loads carried. Consultants were consulted, and even their opinions ignored in one case. Eventually the plunge was taken, and a decision made not to buy proper coaches, but to contract hire them, no doubt in case the ideas did not work out. The first were delivered in 1977, with a

Left: The 90 Park Royal-bodied AEC Reliance coaches shared much of their front-end design with Park Royal Atlantean double-deckers. Two are seen in Harlow on Green Line work.

Right: Early in its independent existence LCBS began to build up a private hire fleet. Here a Plaxton-bodied AEC Reliance, bought secondhand from National Travel (South East) approaches Victoria coach station to take up work as a duplicate on a National Express service.

Below: An unusual secondhand purchase, still with LCBS, was a fleet of ex-Barton Plaxton-bodied AEC Reliances with low-back three-and-two coach seats.

WOKING
LONDON COUNTRY
GREEN LINE
GREEN LINE
GPH 2V

FLIGHTLINE777
LONDON GATWICK
GREEN LINE
SOUTHDOWN
RS136
CY
FLIGHTLINE777
EPM 136V

Left: Before placing a bulk order for Leopards, two were bought with two Volvo B58s; all received Duple bodies. The second Volvo is seen in Dartford.

Below left: At the Leatherhead garage open day, a Plaxton-bodied Reliance in green and gold Flightline 777 livery and joint Southdown fleetname, for the Victoria-Gatwick service.

Right: Leyland Atlanteans are the mainstay of the double-deck fleet. They have Park Royal or Roe bodies. Although this one carries a local identity for the Crawley town services, it has strayed to Croydon.

regular supply since of 30 a year – 15 with Duple and 15 with Plaxton bodies – to gradually replace the RPs and coach-seated Leyland Nationals. The only criticism one can make of the vehicles – which are leased from Kirkby Central – is the poor destination information, something one would think essential for buses on any infrequent service in an area where up to 10 per cent of the population moves each year. To have a vehicle with single-line blind saying 725 Woking and not mentioning Sutton or Kingston or even Croydon seems silly, particularly in these days when lightweight plastic boards could easily be fabricated. Who knows how much more traffic they might win from a population that knew where they were going?

What has revitalised Green Line has been shrewd marketing, with some splendid and varied literature and publicity, and a concentration on holidaymakers, tourists and shoppers. And the boundaries that the old LT country bus department was tied to have, of course, vanished.

You can find Green Lines in Cardiff, or Milton Keynes, or Brighton, to name but a few. They may not offer many old-style commuter journeys into central London like they used to (though at least one has reappeared) but they have gone out and found custom.

Services from London to Windsor were improved as one of the first steps, with a non-stop Summer service hourly from Victoria, and then there has been concentration on London's three main airports, Heathrow, Gatwick and Luton. Heathrow and Gatwick were already linked, but an hourly non-stop service at a premium fare and with the imaginative route number 747 was added. Coaches with a distinctive livery of yellow stripe added to the green and white of ordinary Green Lines were used, and recently have been replaced by Leyland Leopards (now that Reliances are out of production) with another version of the livery. This route now runs at night, too.

Then there's the joint Southdown – LCBS Gatwick-London service, called Flightline 777, and run in competition with the frequent electric rail service between the two points. It is the result of the recent freeing of the licensing laws and has vehicles from both operators in a gold and green livery. You have to look very hard to decide which operator a vehicle belongs to.

Luton and Luton airport are also served and that service looks healthy whenever I look at it.

You cannot really say much about the services to shopping centres such as Brent Cross or Milton Keynes but those to Brighton are worth a mention. They run from Croydon, Westcott and Dorking and various other places and some originally began as excursions. Then they were converted to stage, and more added – again all possible because of recent legislation. The fight with the railways would otherwise have been considerable. Most run on Saturdays once each way, perhaps also on another weekday or more frequently in school holidays. Often not duplication, but triplication with ex-Barton high capacity Reliances and Atlantean double-deckers is required. It all goes to prove that there is still traffic to be found – by the venturesome.

But perhaps Surrey county council has provided one of the most telling assessments of LCBS's present worth. In a report produced last year it looked at the possibility of transferring LT operated services south of Sutton to LCBS, no doubt in similar fashion to changes made a few years ago in the Kingston area. Apparently only about 7 per cent of passengers ride across Sutton on LT's red Daimler Fleetlines to or from destinations nearer London.

Surrey counted LT's operating costs, at August 1981, at 156p a mile, and LCBS's at 117p. Lost mileage from LCBS's nearest garages, at Leatherhead and Reigate, was under 1 per cent.

LCBS has come a long way.

A. MOYES

Contemporary Crosville

On the grounds of size alone, Crosville must surely merit some space to itself in *Buses Annual*. The 1980 National Bus Company Report and Accounts shows its fleet size (991 vehicles) to be exceeded by only one other NBC subsidiary, namely London Country. But further justification comes from the fact that the Crosville Motor Company Ltd was incorporated on 6 May 1906, so that the year in which the text of this *Annual* is being written is the successor's seventy fifth. Its founder, George **Cros**land Taylor, set up the company to assemble car parts in Chester supplied by M Georges **Ville** of Paris, hence the name 'Crosville'. It did not prosper until after bus services, which had commenced in 1911 from Chester to the growing town of Ellesmere Port on the Mersey, overcame their teething troubles. Pre-1914 expansion was slow, and wholly eastwards into Cheshire. But after the First World War a toe-hold was soon established in industrial north-east Wales, followed by pioneering in the Wirral peninsula, and also north eastwards towards Runcorn and Warrington, thence with a pincer movement westwards towards Liverpool. Then in the words of one of the founder's sons, 'we saw the almost untouched area of north Wales, and fell'.

Starting at Llanrwst in 1922, there were depots at Blaenau Ffestiniog, Barmouth, Dolgellau, Llanidloes, Aberystwyth, Llandrindod Wells, and Kington within two years. The intervening ground was gradually filled in by acquisitions, especially after the LMS Railway bought the company in 1929. By 1931, the north Wales coastal strip was almost wholly in Crosville hands. The last major gaps were sealed when Western Transport, a BET subsidiary centred on Wrexham but thinly present elsewhere in north Wales, was acquired. Subsequently, the only significant extensions to Crosville's operating territory have been in NBC days: 1972 brought the transfer of North Western's activities in Cheshire and 119 of its vehicles, and 13 more vehicles of Western Welsh origin and some services in Dyfed. In 1974 it gained some local routes at Warrington at the expense of Lancashire United. So Crosville service buses now operate over a varied swathe of country from Manchester and Liverpool to the Potteries and down through Wales as far as Carmarthen. The set of photographs which follows seeks to capture some of that variety and the mixture of vehicles on offer in the early 1980s.

Chester is a logical place to start; on the racecourse in June 1981 are a pair of the company's stock that were drawn up in a celebratory group at the city's carnival. On the left is one of the company's first Mark 2 Leyland Nationals, intended for the Runcorn Busway, of which more anon. Reversion to the old Chester County Borough 'FM' registration, used almost without exception for new purchases until 1975, is noteworthy. Its neighbour is one of the bare dozen ex-North Western vehicles still in public use at the time of writing: one of five Marshall-bodied Bristol RELL6Ls specially brought over from Macclesfield for the occasion. It would take a keen eye (and ear) to discern anything abnormal about the other ex-NWRCC ECW-bodied RELL6Ls, still at Macclesfield and Northwich, though a pair of the low-roofed versions built for the onetime restricted canal bridge at Dunham may still be at Warrington by the time that this is read. The ex-North Western double-deckers were an interesting bunch and lasted surprisingly long considering their non-standard character. The last Alexander-bodied Dennis Lolines hung on until 1978, the AEC Renown/Park Royals till 1979, and the Daimler Fleetlines with Alexander bodies finally disappear after MAP reductions in 1980 at Congleton. A handful of the Marshall-bodied Bristol RESLs have ended up at Runcorn for ancillary use on the Busway, after brief exiles at Bangor, Wrexham and Aberystwyth.

And here on the next photograph is the Busway, possibly Crosville's operational showpiece. It is a most impressive bus-only road system in a twelve mile long figure-of-eight, linking the old Runcorn town centre by the Mersey, with the Shopping City on the hill, various neighbourhood units in the New Town,

and industrial areas. In June 1981, one of the Bristol RELL6Gs which have served on the Busway since new sets down patrons at the Clifton Road stop quite near to the new depot at Beechwood. It has just passed through one of the bus-actuated traffic lights that give it priority at junctions and allow high average speeds. The first section was opened in October 1971, and the final stretches within the old town were complete by 1978. Busway routes have 'T' prefixed route numbers, a system initiated in 1959 with a different letter for each area. The radiator grille on SRG 187 once bore a 'Farebox' sign – a fare collection system tried on several local routes in the early 1970s; the carrier for this can still be seen. Although Crosville only ever had 175 RE buses (and bus-shell dual purpose specimens) they still seem ubiquitous. As well as intensive urban use, they manage to insinuate themselves down the tiny lanes for which the company, from early days, has had a predeliction. Withdrawals are, however, gaining momentum.

But Crosville's is by no means a wholly sd fleet. Until the mid-1960s, 60 per cent of the stock was dd, thanks to the purchase of some 350 LD-type Bristol Lodekkas between 1953 and 1959. The next eight years produced 30 FSF, 84 FLF and 127 FS variants on the Lodekka theme, the last of these (if Gardner-engined) having been the longest-lived. Not surprisingly, Lodekkas were found throughout the system, from Crewe to Cardigan, Altrincham to Aberdaron. Then with the advent of high-capacity one-man single-deckers, the dd frontier was pushed back. Lodekkas hung on tenaciously at Liverpool until April 1981; only in June that year did Llandudno Junction's FS6Gs succumb (and then with the promise of a final summer at Rhyl); the last at Wrexham were likely to follow soon after. (The future of the last ten Bristol FLF6Gs, all at Bangor for school contracts, is uncertain). In memoriam, here next is a view of a row of back-loaders in Wrexham's Mold Road depot on a Sunday afternoon in April 1980, when there were still 34 FSs allocated. Even after three stages of MAP revisions, surviving Lodekkas were still hammering away on the Chester-Wrexham-Llangollen and Oswestry trunk routes in June 1981, rather than humble duties. Conveniently for this narrative, two other inmates can be seen. DLG 946, an open-top Lodekka in all-white garb, at the end of the line, is one of 14 delivered new in that state. They have had heavy seasonal use at Rhyl and Llandudno Junction depots, but in the winter of 1979-80, several were despatched to unfamiliar spots like Wrexham, for tree-cutting. Also in the distance is a glimpse of the rear of Ford Transit MTF 700, receiving mechanical attention before its next week's work as the Uwchaled Community Bus. Based 35 miles west at Cerrig-y-Druidion, it is operated in the same way as that at Sharrington, Norfolk (see *Buses Annual 1981*). A more modern Reebur-bodied Ford, likewise in National red and white rather than Crosville's National green, replaced it shortly after this photo was taken.

The modern double-decker in the fleet is almost inevitably the Bristol VRT. Crosville's first specimens did not arrive until 1975, and went to Liverpool, where an early example is seen next to the Cunard building at Mann Island, part of the Pier Head. Delivery thereafter was steady, there being some 235 of them in stock, both Gardner- and Leyland-engined, by the end of the model's production. The Liverpool and north Wirral operations have been conducted on behalf of the Merseyside PTE since an agreement in 1972, which guaranteed Crosville 13.07 per cent of vehicle mileage within the PTE area. DVG 280, like others of the 150-odd vehicles allocated to Liverpool, Rock Ferry (Birkenhead) and West Kirby depots in the PTE area, carries both the NBC and Merseyside PTE logos. From Mann Island, there are at least 20 departures per off-peak hour to the east, mainly VRT-operated, but as the photograph shows, Leyland Nationals also appear. Their forte is mainly those routes which were developed crossing the new Widnes-Runcorn bridge in 1961, and which end up in some cases at Chester. Since 1976, VRTs have also entered Liverpool on the lower-frequency Rapidride service from Heswall via the second Mersey tunnel, but these terminate in the city's business district, some way away from the waterfront. On the other side of the river, a major rationalising of Crosville and former Birkenhead and Wallasey municipal routes took place on 1 April 1979, almost obliterating the former pattern of provision.

To accelerate one-man double-decking, the company purchased some second-hand double deckers in 1980 which have provided new variety. First, six Bristol VRT/East Lancs were obtained from South Yorkshire PTE, others of the

same type going simultaneously to Maidstone & District. HVG 934 is seen in a rather different environment from Liverpool, squeezing past the old market hall in Llanidloes, Powys, in April 1981. Crosville has run buses from here since 1924, but for almost 40 years only on a thinnish service beside the Severn to Newtown. At the end of 1962 and again in 1964, the local railway network was cut back, and a little extra work came to Llanidloes depot; some of it, like the rail replacement service to Brecon joint with Western Welsh, was short-lived. Of more permanent significance was Crosville's taking over the most promising routes of Mid Wales Motorways, along with eight staff, in February 1970. These allowed a through service to be created from Llanidloes through Newtown and Welshpool to Shrewsbury. There were enough VRTs available by 1980 to permit double-decking, the individual vehicles circulating between the parent depot at Oswestry, the old Mid Wales patch at Welshpool, and the Crosville yard at Llanidloes. These East Lancs-bodies machines are all either in this Oswestry circuit or at Machynlleth and Aberystwyth. Southdown more recently provided another thirty omo-suitable double-deckers, all Daimler Fleetlines. Half are Northern Counties-bodied, most of them having been concentrated at Wrexham to displace Lodekkas. The others are ECW-bodied; many have gone to Pwllheli and Caernarfon to replace sds and reduce school contract duplication. At the latter they have also, excitingly, appeared on the Snowdon Sherpa summer service thence via the Llanberis pass to Pen-y-gwryd – a magnificent way of seeing north Wales's finest scenery.

For some, particularly route and timetable addicts, Crosville is perhaps the NBC's rural bus company *par excellence.* Thanks partly to £4 million of local authority subsidies, its rural and market-day routes still probe into the crevices of rural Wales and the northern marches. This is despite some reductions especially in the late 1960s and the threat of more, not often achieved, a decade later. Nevertheless, the future of these services remains problematical. Most of the six shire counties in which it operates have policies to encourage the survival of at least a strategic bus network, which should need relatively little revenue support, and to ensure that operators get a good share of school contract work, thereby being able to run off-peak marginally-costed services. The next photograph shows one of the forty Bristol LH6Ls, SLL 615, at work as a school bus *(bws ysgol)* at Rhydlewis, near

Llandyssul, Ceredigion, in February 1981. It was based at Newcastle Emlyn, one of two depots transferred from Western Welsh in 1972, and indeed had been allocated there almost continuously since it was new in 1975, when it helped to oust the last ex-WW Leyland Tiger Cub buses. It bears the local brand name of DeCambria, introduced on all vehicles in Dyfed and at Machynlleth as part of a MAP revamp in January 1980; others elsewhere include Glan Clwyd (Denbigh) and TransPort (Ellesmere Port). Rhydlewis has not had a Crosville public bus since 1973, but a little further north, four other onetime-Western Welsh contracts from Aberaeron school have been made public. The LH type may not last much longer; an earlier Perkins-engined batch has already gone, along with thirteen bought from United Counties in 1979.

Crosville has of course more prestigious routes. The prime limited-stop venture is undoubtedly the hourly L1 express along the north Wales coast from Chester to Caernarfon. This began in August 1965 with Bristol RELH coaches and semi-coaches, and with dd Lodekka coaches cascaded down from express services proper. Now it usually produces Leyland National dual purpose vehicles, such as ENL 922, seen approaching Bangor's Town Clock terminal in October 1981, with University College of North Wales looming above it. This highly successful route supplements stopping services between the same points which were nominally linked together in 1965 but dismembered at Llandudno and Rhyl in 1976, largely because of traffic congestion. Crosville received almost 270 series A, podded Nationals between 1972 and 1979, roughly half of them buses, the other half dual-purpose. They spread widely among depots in England, Clwyd and north Gwynedd; only recently have some filtered further south. There they reinforce representatives of the 85 B series variants which arrived from 1978 to clear out the last of the Bristol MW6G saloons. Other daily limited stop services include the Townlynx network centred on the knot of motorways in north Cheshire, which began in December 1979 and has transmuted itself into a Chester-Manchester axis, worked by specially-liveried Leyland Leopard/Duple coaches.

When National Travel's Central Activities Group was established in 1972, Crosville's coaches assumed the all-white livery. Among the express routes the most important were those between Liverpool and London. These had started in 1927 and were buttressed by taking over Ribble's interest in this route in 1931, then that of the Red & White group in 1934, and finally Messrs Pearson, Jones and Horne in 1936. These, and some others, passed to National Travel (West) in March 1980 along with five newish Leopard/Duple coaches. Other less regular, mostly summer only facilities were built up to Welsh resorts from within Crosville's operating area. The mid-1960s saw once-weekly services starting from Welsh depots to Manchester and Liverpool (and in one case, Swansea).

Bearing NT route numbers, a pair of 1969 Bristol RELH6G coaches enter Aberystwyth depot in August 1978 on the next picture, respectively on routes 973 from Rhyl and 974 from Bangor, whose backgrounds can be traced to 1939. They were part of a host of early Saturday afternoon arrivals that would form departures at 14.30hrs or thereabouts, of mini-Cheltenham character. Thereby, traffic between north Wales, Manchester, Birmingham, south Wales and Bristol was exchanged. The level of summer express services here was reduced greatly in 1981. The first Traws Cambria services were begun in 1979 linking Bangor and Cardiff, and these provide a similar connectivity as before, on more days per week but involving more changes than through services. Aberystwyth depot, built in 1934, typifies those of the more rural areas. It was built for 35 vehicles, accumulated from acquisitions from local independents and routes pioneered by the Great Western and Corris railways, as well as by Crosville itself.

The last two illustrations serve to symbolise the contrasts in Crosville's operating territory, from the Cheshire plain on the one hand to Snowdonia on the other. First, in July 1979, barely one

hundred feet above sea level at Crewe depot we have SPG 785, one of the surviving Seddon Pennine buses, one of 50 dual-doorway machines delivered in 1971 and 1972. The fifty dual-purpose versions have not been quite so heavily withdrawn yet, although they are not as generally popular as Bristol REs. Another dying breed is represented at the rear by DFG 255, one of the last 20 Bristol Lodekkas delivered to Crosville, in 1968. When new, it plied on the Chester – Newcastle-u-Lyme trunk route; as mentioned earlier, the surviving forward-entrance Lodekkas are all at the time of writing at Bangor. Crewe was largely switched to omo sd operation in the early 1970s, but dds reasserted themselves late in 1980: hired VRTs from South Wales Transport! The towcar here is an ex-NWRCC Leopard/Alexander.

At the other topographic extreme, Leyland National B SNL662 was witnessed in Manod, a tentacle of the slate-mining town of Blaenau Ffestiniog, on a scholars' short working on the Tanygrisiau-Blaenau-Pwllheli service in October 1981. It bears the 'Bws Lyn' label, and publicity for the Gwynedd Dayrider ticket, which gives almost unlimited county-wide bus travel for £1.95 per day.

Blaenau attracted Crosville in 1924, with a service down the steep hill to Porthmadog and then across Arfon to Pwllheli. The local service to Tanygrisiau was acquired from Davies Bros in 1937. It covers a remarkably tortuous narrow road, and was coupled to the Pwllheli service following subsidy negotiations with Gwynedd County Council in 1976, a pattern remaining, though thinned by MAP. The climax of operation at Blaenau Ffestiniog must surely be route R40. This runs seasonally from former slate mines and quarries on the north edge of town now devoted to tourism, to the Festiniog Railway's present terminus at Tanygrisiau and then, since 1964, up the searing, tortuous climb to the Stwlan dam. This, part of a pump storage power station, lies on the upper flanks of the Moelwyn mountains at almost 1700 ft above sea level. This is probably an appropriate high point on which to leave Crosville; given this variety it is perhaps not surprising that it has attracted a large band of enthusiastic devotees in the shape of the very active Crosville Enthusiasts Club (1967), whose newsletters, directly and indirectly, have been a great help in preparing this necessarily selective story.

On the Greyhound Track

The world-famous Greyhound organisation has been providing a network of long-distance coach services in North America for more than 50 years. Greyhound coaches have always set high standards in comfort and design, and these photographs trace their development over the last three decades.

One of the most dramatic Greyhound designs was the Super Scenicruiser. A thousand of these distinctive coaches were built between 1954 and 1956, exclusively for Greyhound. Manufactured by GMC and designated PD4501, they originally had two four-cylinder engines to provide sufficient power, but in 1961/2 they were rebuilt with Detroit Diesel 8V-71 engines. They were used by Greyhound until the mid-1970s.

Following Greyhound's acquisition of Motor Coach Industries, a Canadian builder, a series of MCI models have been built. The MC-6 was only built in 1969/70 – 100 coaches exclusively for Greyhound – but its 8ft 6in width restricted its use to certain states. Originally with 12-cylinder engines, they later received 8V-71s, and are now withdrawn.

The MCI MC-7 *(top)* was built from 1968-73, featuring a high floor to provide extra luggage space under the floor. Like all recent Greyhound coaches the MC-7 is 40ft by 8ft, with a rear-mounted V8-71 engine. It was succeeded by the highly-popular MC-8 *(above),* dubbed Americruiser. Current from 1973-78, more than 2,600 were built. The current model is the MC-9 *(right),* with flatter roof line and squared-off windows. MCI coaches are available commercially, built in Canada, while Greyhound's production is centred at the Transport Manufacturing Corporation at Roswell, New Mexico.

Welsh Memories

Photographs by R. L. WILSON

South Wales offered great municipal variety in the 1950s and 1960s. The maroon and cream Aberdare UDC fleet included three of these 1951 AEC Regent III with Northern Counties bodies. Aberdare became Cynon Valley in 1974.

A similar bus in the tiny Bedwas & Machen UDC fleet (dark blue and cream). This undertaking disappeared into Rhymney Valley.

In the green and cream Caerphilly UDC fleet, a 1944 Guy Arab II with 55-seat Roe utility body. Caerphilly, too, was merged into Rhymney Valley.

The Cardiff municipal fleet remains, although not in the crimson and cream worn by this 1938 AEC Regent, with 7.7 litre engine and preselective gearbox. One of a batch of ten, it carried 56-seat Northern Counties coachwork. It was withdrawn in 1957.

Colwyn Bay, now simply Colwyn, always had a tiny bus fleet. In 1961 it operated this green and cream Bedford J2LZ2 with Spurling 21-seat body, new the previous year.

In the smart green, red and grey livery of Gelligaer UDC, a brand new Leyland Titan PD2/40 with 55-seat lowbridge Longwell Green body seen in 1959. The wheel-nut guard ring is to an unusual design. Gelligaer was the third fleet to merge into Rhymney Valley.

Llandudno UDC (now Aberconwy) used this 1951 Metalcraft-bodied Foden PVSC6 on the climb to Great Ormes Head. It was painted maroon and cream, and is seen in 1953 at Llandudno Town Hall.

Merthyr Tydfil Corporation survives as the Borough Council undertaking, though not in the maroon and cream carried by this 1956 Leyland Titan PD2/12 with 60-seat Longwell Green body, one of three.

The Newport name also survives, and the buses are still green and cream. Six of these all-Leyland Titan PD2/3s were delivered in 1949 – Newport's first 8ft wide buses.

To help with Pontypridd UDC's trolleybus replacement, three of these Guy Arab LUFs with 41-seat Roe rear-entrance bodies were bought in 1957. It is seen where new in the navy blue and cream livery. Today the undertaking is Taff Ely.

A once-famous bus, the Leyland Alpine Beaver TSC9 of the West Monmouthshire Omnibus Board. New in 1935, it received this Burlingham 32-seat utility body in 1944. Painted chocolate and cream, it was bought for the notorious Bargoed Hill climb. West Mon is now Islwyn.

Not a bus-operating authority in the strictest sense, but Hawarden Rural District Council, in Flintshire, had this 1949 ex-Blackpool Leyland Titan PD2/3 in 1970 for use by its Architect and Surveyor's Department. It carried distinctive Burlingham 54-seat centre-entrance bodywork.

Buses from Bretherton

JOHN E. DUNABIN

This 36hp Leyland, CK 3174, was new to Mr Jump in 1920, and was originally a charabanc/lorry convertible.

In 1919 Mr John Bamford Jump of Bretherton bought his first motor bus, an ex-WD Leyland. With it he ran market day services to Preston, eight miles away, and other towns within relatively easy reach of his base, Chorley, Ormskirk, Southport, and Wigan. He continued to serve the public, with more modern vehicles, while many independent bus owners in the area he covered came and went, until the end of 1939. Mr Jump however was more firmly based than these birds of passage, having graduated from horse bus operation over some of the same roads. His 'Bus Work Book' for 1914-1915, which has recently come into the writer's possession, although primarily a straightforward record of receipts, does yield additional information about the nature of Mr Jump's business before mechanisation.

Regular journeys were made to Chorley on Tuesdays, Ormskirk on Thursdays, and Preston on Saturdays. One bus, as was usual on such services, met passenger demand for Ormskirk and Preston – greater numbers usually produced a second supplier – but the Chorley service not infrequently called for duplication. Variety came in here, with sometimes a second bus, sometimes a cab (presumably a horse-drawn one), and on other occasions a 'float'. The 'dittoing' in Mr Jump's book, indicating duplication, is probably a less reliable indication of its extent than the receipts for the journey. When two buses were specifically mentioned they rose to over £2-0-0; at other times the figure was usually between £1-5-0 and £1-10-0, although with a cab or float to help it climbed a little higher.

Receipts on the Ormskirk service were on average much lower, and fluctuated considerably. One of the poorest weeks in 1914, with only 5-6d (gross) for Mr Jump, was preceded by one when fourteen shillings were collected. This low week could have resulted from wintry weather, but fluctuating weather conditions can hardly explain a rise from 6/- on July 2 to £1-3-0 on July 9. It could have been that there was a special market on the latter date, but the pattern was not repeated in 1915. August of 1915 was a good month, with receipts of over £1-0-0 on each trip. What though of August 1914, that most momentous time? Two higher than average collections came from Ormskirk-bound passengers on the 13th and 20th, and a higher than average amount on the Chorley run (with a cab to help) on August 11, but then, the corresponding weekend of 1915 produced an even more noticeable peak, calling for two buses.

One cannot tell whether receipts accurately mirrored varying demand, or whether there was an upper (variable) limit, dependent on availability of vehicles and horses. And did passengers have to book in advance?

Receipts from Preston journeys were steadier, and on average came between those for the other two venues. Here there was also some traffic in parcels, clearly unaccompanied ones, a Mr Gardener being named as consignor (or consignee; the record is unhelpful on this point) on several occasions. Numbers varied up to

Another of Mr Jump's Leylands, photographed in Ormskirk. Note the hampers on the roof and the amply garbed ladies waiting below.

three per trip.

A week's takings from all three services could be as little as £2-10-0, and in 1914 the average was below £3-0-0.

The possibility of wintry weather reducing patronage has been mentioned. I have not checked the newspaper files to establish whether the winters of 1914 and 1915 were such as to hamper movement in West Lancashire or not. The record commences on January 6, and from then on Mr Jump completed his 155 scheduled journeys in 1914, wind and weather notwithstanding.

Apart from regular journeys there was also what Mr Jump merely called 'Extra Bus Work', essentially what would now be described as private hire or charter. Here one can learn more about numbers carried and fares charged. Pricing policy appeared to be a compromise between two extremes, one based on vehicle miles and the other on passenger miles. On January 20, 1914, 21 persons were conveyed to the Farmers' Ball – and back home one assumes – for 1/3d each, but how long a journey this entailed is not stated. The next entry, dated January 24, is equally unhelpful in this respect. Eleven footballers were conveyed to Holmeswood for eleven shillings, but where from? The next 'Extra' however ran from Croston to Rufford, a distance of 3½ miles. For this journey, a return journey one must again assume, 20 people each paid eightpence.

Footballers were specifically mentioned in connection with the January 24 (Saturday) trip, but not again in 1914, although on Saturday February 14, 12 persons (team plus one reserve?) were conveyed 5½ miles from Croston to Holmeswood for ten shillings, and the same amount was charged for a seven-mile journey to Holmes on Saturday March 7. In 1915 Croston footballers were conveyed to Tarleton and to Leyland on successive Saturdays in January, and to Tarleton again in April. Without the 1914 information, this limited demand might have been assumed to be the result of some wartime limitation; perhaps it just was that the football season, for amateurs at least, was normally shorter than it is now.

But although 'Extra Work' only amounted to 20 jobs in 1914 and thirteen in 1915, there was much more to it than merely carrying footballers. Miss Fowler's wedding in May 1914 called for two trips to Croston station, while Mrs Howard's funeral on March 10 resulted in two trips being made to different destinations, Walmer Bridge and Longton. Then there were school excursions, conveyance of choirs, and journeys to Southport for various reasons, including one on August 12, 1914 when 'Milk' was referred to, without explanation or qualification. Mr Jump was first and foremost a farmer; did he provide liquid refreshment on this occasion?

Perhaps though the most interesting extras are those for July 7 and 8, 1915, 'To Southport with a party of friends from Burnley', and on the following day, 'To Riding a party out from Preston by Rufford, Holmeswood and Bretherton'. If the entry has been correctly deciphered, they got a bargain at a shilling each, although they may have been squashed together, since the total sum of £1-0-0 indicates that there were 20 of them.

The last entry in Mr Jump's book, an isolated one for July 28 (the year was probably 1916), reads 'To Blackpool from Hesketh Bank'. The charge for this much longer than usual run was £7-0-0.

With the advent of motors Mr Jump intensified his service, and when a second powered vehicle had been acquired he was able to serve many points he had not covered with his horse buses. On Mondays two buses ran to Preston in the early afternoon, one skirting Leyland, while the other, which actually started at Mawdesley, went via Hoole and Longton. Tuesday was Chorley market day, and again two buses were in service, one running through Mawdesley and Croston, the other via Ulnes Walton and Runshaw Moor. One bus only was needed for advertised service on Wednesday, to run from Bretherton via Croston, Mawdesley, and Rufford to Southport.

Two buses were required again on Thursdays for Ormskirk, one going via Tarleton and the other through Holmeswood. While waiting to return some hours later, one or both of them ran something like a 'shuttle' service over the three-mile long section between Burscough and Ormskirk. Mr Jump began and remained as a market busman, and did not become involved in the fierce struggles for passengers which occurred some miles further north in the Preston/Chorley/Leyland triangle, but here he certainly had a competitor in Mr Fishwick of Leyland, who also had a bus idle in Ormskirk on market days, and ran a very similar shuttle.

Market going for many people has always meant getting up early, but none of the services mentioned up to now started before 11.30am. Wigan market-goers had to rise much earler however. One bus left Bretherton at 7.25am and ran in via Mawdesley and Wrightington, while the other, catering for later risers, followed at 8.40, running instead through Eccleston. This one additionally had two short workings between Mawdesley and Wigan.

Saturday was however the big day of the week, with four journeys to Wigan via Mawdesley (two starting at Bretherton, two at Croston), and four to Preston, three of these running via Longton and one via Leyland and Tardy Gate. On Sundays a similar service (with some small timing changes) to that of Saturday was operated to Wigan, but no other routes were covered.

Altogether then, the people of the village of Bretherton wishing to travel had many choices open to them. In the middle 1920s Mr Albert Dallas of Earnshaw Bridge established a daily bus service between Croston and Preston via Bretherton and Longton, while Ribble Motor Services, expanding rapidly, ran more frequently past Bretherton Road Toll House, less than a mile from the village, between Preston and Southport and between Preston and Ormskirk for Liverpool, but Mr Jump, offering a more personal service, held his own.

The business, farming and running buses, became a family one, Mr Jump being joined by his two sons, John and Peter. His son-in-law, Mr Rigby, was a regular driver, helping on the farm when not so occupied, and Mrs Rigby conducted. The buses were garaged in Mr Jump's barn.

The services were maintained for the first few months of the war, but from January 1, 1940, by agreement with Mr Jump and his two sons, Ribble Motor Services Ltd took them over. The family were then able to concentrate on farming.

Buses still run through Bretherton several times each weekday, with room for all who want to travel (by bus that is) to Croston or Preston, but of the many routes and destinations offered by Mr Jump, albeit infrequently, few are now served by this means.

Mr Jump's daughter, Mrs Rigby, who conducted for her husband. The vehicle behind is an AEC Regal, new in 1930 to Smiths (Safeways) of Middlesbrough.

Right: The familiar and much-loved Burlingham Seagull coach body, one of the first examples to be seen in Gloucestershire, here on a Sodbury Queen Leyland Royal Tiger, leaving Yatesbury RAF Station.

Travel by Sodbury Queen

EDWARD DAVIS recalls a Gloucestershire coach operator.

One morning in 1921, a 17-year old Gloucestershire boy was given ten minutes driving instruction and was then sent off at the wheel of a Ford Model T truck to deliver a load of coal. In 1948 Mr Richard Febry's resulting haulage company was nationalised and so he thought he would try his hand at coaches instead. In fact the company had run a few coaches for local workmens' services etc. and so were not absolute beginners in the field.

Accordingly their new coaches were delivered to them, the first being a Maudslay with bodywork by Whitehorns of Bristol and supplied by Dando's of Chipping Sodbury; a real local effort. Next came a Dennis Lancet supplied by Windmill & Lewis of Bristol. Both were in the soon-to-be familiar off-white and blue livery of Febry's Sodbury Queen coaches and boasted the fact that they were 'Radio Luxury Coaches' along the sides of the roof. The name 'Sodbury Queen' originated from the landlady of a local public house whom Richard Febry's father called 'Queenie'!

The next acquisitions were a Foden Diesel half cab – remembered as the first coach seen in the area with the new 'modern' full width engine compartment and car-style radiator grille – and a 25-seat Bedford OB.

My own memories of Febry's coaches as a young boy in the early 1950s are of annual outings of the local church choir of which I was a member. Sunday School outings were mundane affairs, usually to Weston-super-Mare and always in coaches of a rival firm who only ran Guy Vixens – very inferior to our childish eyes. Choir outings however were an entirely different story; we went on long journeys to such exotic destinations as Bournemouth and Swanage, or Teignmouth and Dawlish, or even Torquay, and more important we always had Sodbury Queen coaches and they were so much posher! In fact by this time Febry's were one of the first firms in the area to run coaches with underfloor engines – streamlined affairs with big curved windscreens, long front overhangs and even some Harringtons with tailfins – this was living indeed.

The first of these underfloor engined coaches and indeed another first in the area was a Leyland Royal Tiger with

RADIO LUXURY COACH
RADIO LUXURY COACH

PRIVATE
RADIO LUXURY COACH
KAD 273

Left: Leyland PS2s with Plaxton bodies at Yatesbury.

Above: The Foden with 41-seat Plaxton body leaves Yatesbury, as Mr Bill Febry looks on.

Burlingham Seagull bodywork.

All the coaches were beautifully turned out in the off-white and blue livery, now with a smart logo on the sides with a map of Great Britain in a circle and the legend 'Travel by Sodbury Queen'. Of course they had 'Radio Luxury Coach' above the windows. The rival firm tried to go one better with the slogan 'Radio Luxury Heater Coach' but it was still only a Vixen and we were not impressed.

Besides organised outings as described, Febry's were expanding their coach operations in a big way, with contract work for local factories such as Newman Industries, transporting local school children to the various secondary schools (we lived almost on the doorstep of our school so I was never so lucky as to ride Sodbury Queen to school) and transporting RAF personnel to and from Yatesbury Air Station.

Many excursions were also run on summer weekends. Destinations included London (17s 0d return), Bournemouth or Weymouth (10s 0d return) and Weston-super-Mare (5s 0d). By this time Febry's had 30 coaches of their own, all purchased brand-new, but they would hire up to 70 more from other local operators at busy weekends. At times like this the line of coaches on a Saturday morning would run from their yard in Chipping Sodbury right through to Yate Railway Station almost a mile away.

The sheer logistics of preparing a line of 100 coaches like this is almost beyond imagining. The standard of maintenance in the vehicles was very high; each had to be cleaned (they were always spotless, inside and out); they had to be fuelled and provided with a driver who had to be briefed with route, time schedule etc. Not a job for the faint-hearted!

The 1950s were in fact the heyday of Sodbury Queen coaches. After 1959 this side of the business began to be run down as lorries once again became more important to the company. The last coaches ran in 1969 but the name of R. & W. Febry still lives on as one of the major haulage contractors in the West Country; indeed, you see Febry's lorries everywhere.

In conclusion I would like to express my thanks to Mr Richard Febry for his help in preparing this article and for providing the photographs from his collection.

Gone for Scrap

Photographs by T. W. MOORE

Barnsley is Britain's bus graveyard. To this part of South Yorkshire thousands of buses have made their last journey.

The family concern of Wombwell Diesels break up buses for their living. Buses are carefully stripped of engines, gearboxes and chassis parts. There is a brisk worldwide trade in these items.

Wombwell Diesels have also resold buses, to all parts of the world – the Far East, South Africa, Europe, Canada, as well as to the home second-hand market.

But for the buses that have really reached the end of the road, there is no mercy. It is a sobering sight for an enthusiast: the dismantling gangs smash and cut on all sides; buses are stripped to sorry skeletons, reduced to wrecks and battered into scrap iron.

The scrap finally goes to refuel the steel industry at nearby Sheffield.

But although the business is bus-breaking, the Wombwell men are always quietly pleased to see a bus leave under its own power – en route for restoration.

Framed by a wheel in the corner of the yard, an ex-Southport Leyland TD3 with open-top English Electric body.

Upright, though mutilated – a former London Transport Metropolitan (MD128) at Wombwell Diesels. New in 1976, it is seen in 1981.

Who's next? Former London Transport RTs (left to right) 379, 2146, 3254, 4770 and 2150. Bruised by the weather in their long silence at Wombwell, awaiting their doom in August 1981.

Right: Mere skeletons of their former selves, former London RTs 3840 and 1654, framed by an ex Hartlepool Borough Leyland PD2/40 with Roe body, of 1965.

Above: Two ex-Green Line Routemasters, 1455 and 1478, have been stripped before dismantling for spares for London Transport in 1981.

Below: A line of ex-London RFs await their fate in 1981. Seen are RFs 448, 432, 519, 334, 687 and 513.

Darkness hangs over the future of an ex-Green Line SMA class AEC Swift with Alexander body, dumped after panel stripping.

Reflecting a scene of destruction, three of the ill-fated London Transport SM class Park Royal-bodied AEC Swifts.

The end for a Daimler Fleetline SRG6 with Pennine body, KCP 379G. New in 1969 to Halifax Corporation, it was latterly West Yorkshire PTE 3109. It is seen in 1980 being bulldozed on to the pile after all useful body parts had been removed.

In the stockpile of buses and coaches awaiting breaking at Wombwell in September 1980 was 1914 WA, a 1960 Leyland Leopard L1 with Weymann body new to Sheffield Corporation. It was latterly with Stevensons of Spath, as number 28.

Titan Tattoo

D. FEREDAY GLENN

The two former Southdown Leyland Titan TD1s pause for breath at Droxford Square.

On the face of it, there did not appear to be anything very unusual about Saturday, June 13 1981. The day had dawned dull and grey – like so many others before and since – but had brightened during the morning to become sunny and warm by lunchtime. If you will excuse my mixing metaphors, this was to be only the tip of a melting iceberg. . .

Imagine relaxing on the slopes of Portsdown Hill after lunch on such a day, with no more than the distant hum of traffic in the city below like the sound of a swarm of contented bees. Some way off, a different timbre can be discerned: a sort of controlled, metallic scream such as one has not heard for 30 years in this place, the kind of sound to make the pulse quicken and stir all manner of strange memories of bygone days. Looking down towards the entrance to Queen Alexandra's Hospital at the foot of Southwick Hill Road, where half a century ago the green trams ascended Portsdown on a girder bridge on their way to Horndean, a quaint old open-top bus emerges from the trees to glint in the sunlight. Painted in brilliant green and cream, the boldly shaded block letters on its flank proclaim the name SOUTHDOWN. But what is this? Beyond this vision of the past appears another vehicle, a tall double-decker with arched roof and similar livery, practically as old as the first and emitting the same distinctive transmission note as it grapples with the challenge of a 1 in 10 gradient.

Steadily they battle their way up the long straight slope to the roundabout at the top, whence they disappear from view back into the dream-world of forgotten memories. Even after they have disappeared from sight, the distinctive exhaust backfiring can be heard on the descent to Southwick to prove this was no cruel deceit of the imagination. But didn't the destination indicator read '38', whereas everyone knows these days it is service 350 for Southwick and Wickham? And didn't the second bus say 'Relief' – since when have they been running extras on Saturdays, except when Pompey play at home at Fratton Park? It must have been a dream. . .

To be brutally frank, dear reader, this was no dream. It was the culmination of six months' negotiation with the bus company (as owner of the open-topper) and Michael Plunkett (owner/driver of the second veteran) by Clive Wilkin and myself and, for the writer at least, the realisation of a 15-year ambition to bring a petrol Titan back to Portsmouth. But let us follow the progress of that ancient pair as they roam the highways and byways of East Hampshire and West Sussex that summer afternoon. On arrival in Southwick village for a photo-stop, all hell was let loose with the unexpected arrival of a Leyland National working the 350 back to Portsmouth! Cottage doors were flung open, locals gaped at the unwonted sight of no less than three Southdown buses in their midst – for ten minutes the place became distinctly busy and the solitary shop did a roaring trade in canned drinks and sweets. Order was restored by the National squeezing between the serried ranks of parked cars, thereby making room for the more compact transport of the 1930s to continue on its nostalgic way to Wickham. Passing Boarhunt Garage, where buses had been based before Blue Motors was absorbed by Southdown in 1935, the pair soon reached Wickham Square for the second photo-stop. Contact was renewed with Hants & Dorset, as in days of yore, before retreating to the less populated villages of Soberton and Droxford.

Following a brief pause at Droxford's historic railway station and an about-turn in the Square, the two veterans climbed on to the downs for a pleasant run to Hambledon (noted not only for cricket but also as an early outpost for Southdown in the pioneering days of 1920). Passing the present depot with its solitary VRT inside, we rambled on at a gentle 20-25mph to Clanfield before low-gear work was required again near Leydene. After the magical climb through the trees there came the delightful descent to the picturesque East Meon, its church spire clearly marking the next point on our itinerary and the erstwhile limit of Southdown influence (summer Sundays extension of the 140). By popular acclaim there was another photo-stop, with an opportunity to check radiator levels after steam had been seen to emerge during the woodland interlude, but all was well. The buses slipped unobtrusively through the Hants & Dorset 'corridor' to Petersfield, where more heads than usual were turned on account of its being market-day. A brief pause by the War Memorial to retrieve those who had gone ahead to take pictures, before continuing past the Heath and its lake for a run out to

Looking strange with temporary canvas roof in position, a Portsmouth area TD1 of Southdown waits outside Havant Station about 1947.

Flashback – South Harting in 1932 looked very sleepy, nestling in a fold of the Downs. This new Southdown Titan TD1 (937: UF 8377) has been turned round in readiness for the long journey back to Southsea.

Flashback – Posed for the camera half a century ago, an ex-Gosport & Fareham tramcar (renumbered 2 in the Portsdown & Horndean Light Railway fleet in 1930), flanked by brand-new Southdown TD1s 930 and 927 near Purbrook. Both buses were bodied by Short Bros.

Until the late 1940s, the Ship & Bell Horndean marked the terminus of service 41 from Southsea via Fratton, the bus turning round in the yard beside the inn. Preserved 813 and 873 recapture the spirit of those days, with Gales Brewery in the background.

Turning in Droxford Square has been a Southdown tradition since acquiring the service from Blue Motors in 1935. There is little to suggest that this picture was not taken in the mid-1930s – only the TV aerial and timetable case.

Flashback – Before the road-widening on the corner outside the Ship & Bell, at Horndean, Southdown Leyland TD5 173 cautiously negotiates the bend. It carries a 1944 East Lancs body.

South Harting. Some information about our nostalgic journey had been published the day before in the local newspaper *(The News)*, with the result that quite large numbers of sightseers were encountered at several places en route. One elderly lady with clear recollections of the 1930s had waited an hour to see us at Petersfield – her enthusiasm was duly rewarded with a ride to South Harting and back, part of it on the top deck!

It was interesting to recall that South Harting had once been the outpost of a route from Southsea (forerunner of the 42, now 743, between the Coast and Petersfield). As the two old buses purred steadily along between the Downs, so smooth and quiet that the only evidence of effort was the gentle hiss from the carburettor, the dream-like quality of the occasion returned: it was as if time had been suspended and we had drifted back 50 years for the afternoon, sunshine and all. There was no need to hurry and, for once, it seemed as if we had all the time in the world. One reflected that Southdown's own TD1, 813 (UF 4813), had been retired in 1951 after 22 years' active service to join a small group of tree-loppers. By some lucky chance it had been tucked away in a corner of the Works and not sold or scrapped like the

Flashback – to Hilsea Garage, where the journey started. On a wet winter day in the 1950s Southdown 507, one of only a dozen Guy Arab III with Northern Counties bodywork, heads south on the 38 service to Portsmouth.

rest of the 1929 Brush-bodied batch, until sporadic rallying in the 1960s led to its re-instatement as a part-time psv in 1972. Michael Plunkett's machine had been equally fortunate: built as an all-Leyland Hybridge product in 1930, No 873 (UF 6473) spent its entire life with Southdown at Worthing until sold in 1938. After some years at Greenock it became a store inside a warehouse until recovered from Scotland by its present owner. Although woefully shorn of much of its equipment and fittings, the recent renaissance bears witness to a remarkable re-incarnation.

With the Heath in sight once more, the buses prepared to turn south for the assault on Butser. The old London to Portsmouth road has lost many of its distinguishing features but little of its charm over the years, but if Cannonball Corner is now a gentle bend the northern ramp still presents quite a pull for a vehicle as venerable as a Leyland Titan TD1. Modern traffic roared past on the dual carriageway, but there was no hesitation on the veterans' part – in fact, they seemed to be going better than ever. Cars hooted enthusiastically and people waved or flashed their lights in impromptu greeting just as, earlier in the afternoon, groups of onlookers and photographers had gathered at likely places to see these relics from the past. It put one in mind of a double-headed steam-hauled excursion on British Rail!

On a sudden impulse a photo-stop was called for outside the Ship & Bell Inn at Horndean, with Gales Brewery for a backdrop; in the small yard alongside, service 41 buses had terminated for many years on journeys from Southsea via Fratton Bridge. Plodding on in their unhurried fashion, familiar destinations were passed along the A3 – Cowplain (where the Light Railways Depot had been built in 1902), Waterlooville, Purbrook, Widley and finally Portsdown Hill with the splendid panorama of Portsmouth spread out below. At Hilsea some reluctantly took their leave, but for the rest there was a last extravaganza in the brilliant sunshine as the Titan twosome pulled up at South Parade Pier amidst all the modern machinery. Given the opportunity, there would soon have been a standing load for another trip to Petersfield. . .

With photographers still jostling for position, the time had come to take the Titans back to Hilsea in preparation for the following day's Southsea Spectacular Rally on The Common. As each started without fuss, one was again conscious of the slight hiss from the carburettor and the simple efficiency, regardless of age. A cursory examination of the fuel gauge indicated that consumption was around 7mpg (petrol), a figure that equated well with a modern National (diesel). Having reached the Pier via Fratton Bridge, we returned via Commercial Road and Kingston Crescent, the transmission echoing back from the buildings and singing in one's ears, to be forever impressed upon the memory. And so a unique afternoon's entertainment came to its conclusion for Driver Fisher and his 29 passengers at Hilsea coach station, a good time being had by all. The abiding impression was inescapable: whereas one solitary vintage bus of itself may not seem particularly remarkable, a brace of them can cause a sensation!

The picturesque village of East Meon plays host to the intrepid Titans while revealing an oft-forgotten rear view of the pair.

United Variety

Photographs by G. COXON

For various reasons, United Auto has bought or hired a number of vehicles from other NBC companies. This ex Southern Vectis Bristol LHS6L with Marshall 35-seat body, was one of two acquired in 1977. It was bought for operating over narrow country roads, and is seen at Ripon on the North Yorkshire Flexibus service.

Below: One of eight ex-Crosville Bristol MW6Gs with 43-seat ECW bodies acquired in 1976. They operated in their original green livery most of their operating days in the north-east.

Another Bristol MW6G, this time with 43 seats in an ECW bus shell. It was acquired from Midland General in 1976, and is seen at Durham bus station.

The Bristol FSF6B was always a fairly rare beast, and West Yorkshire's example was transferred to United in 1967. It is seen at Scarborough.

On July 22, 1979, United's Durham garage suffered a disastrous fire, and many vehicles were hired in at short notice. Above are three of the 13 that were loaned by other NBC fleets: Cumberland 111, a Bristol LH6P with ECW 45-seat body; Ribble 679, a Leyland Leopard PSU4/4R with Marshall 44-seat body; and Lincolnshire 1653, a Bristol LH6P with ECW 41-seat body.

United acquired nine of these Ribble Leyland Leopard PSU3/3RT with Plaxton Panorama 49-seat bodies, in 1976. A single-piece doorway ensured that a conductor was always in attendance.

Vanished Bodies

MICHAEL DRYHURST remembers one-time double-deck bodybuilders.

As I sit writing this in Santa Monica, California, overlooking the Pacific Ocean, it is very difficult to recall Britain. It is even more difficult to visualise a Britain where there were over 40 firms building double-decker bus bodies, but such was the case in the late 1940s and 1950s. The postwar boom in road passenger transport prompted a number of companies to enter the double-deck field, although none of these firms now remain in coachbuilding, including some of the large, well-known concerns. This article is a brief review of some of the companies whose double-deck products were on offer in the bus industry in the 15-year period from 1945-1960.

In the south east suburbs of London, **John C. Beadle** of Dartford was a coachbuilder of long-standing, having built many bodies of all types for the Tilling group of companies. The Beadle double-decker of the postwar years was virtually unaltered from the design of the prewar days (Beadle also built wartime austerity bodies to this design), and was of six-bay construction. At a time when the RT design, with its four-bay construction, was influencing most styles, the Beadle body looked decidly dated but nevertheless most distinctive! The Tilling group deliveries were usually early Titan TD1 or TD2 chassis with new lowbridge bodies, although Eastern National had some Regents so bodied, whilst Southdown took delivery of both high- and lowbridge bodies from Beadle, on rebodied Leyland TD3, TD4 and TD5 chassis. In South Wales, Pontypridd Urban District Council also took both double-deck types from the Dartford company, on Bristol K-type chassis. Beadle did not build any double-deck bodies during the early 1950s, concentrating instead on the semi-chassisless rebuilds using AEC Regal/Regent, Leyland Tiger/Titan components that were produced as coaches for the BET group and then on the chassisless coach and saloon design using the Tilling-Stevens developed Rootes TS3 diesel. However, in 1956 Beadle bodied a dozen Leyland Titan PD2/12 for Southdown, these enclosed platform buses being similar in style to the Park Royal bodies being delivered to the Brighton operator at that time. These were the last double-deckers built by Beadle, whose earlier products included two Bristol trolleybus chassis (the only ones ever built) bodied in 1931.

In the Manchester suburb of Wythenshawe was the bodybuilding firm of **Bond,** who supplied a number of northern municipal operators with double-deck bodies,

The main customers for Bond double-deck bodies were Ashton and Bolton, the latter taking 10 on Leyland PD2 chassis, while Ashton took both trolleybus and bus bodies, a 60-seat Guy Arab IV being seen here.

including Ashton and Bolton, the former taking both buses and trolleybuses. The Ashton buses were Guy Arab IVs with exposed radiators, and BUT 9613T trolleybuses, whilst the Bolton examples were on Leyland Titan chassis. In Scotland, **Brockhouse** supplied a number of operators with bodywork, including double-deckers on Albion chassis for Glasgow Corporation, AEC Regent IIIs for Edinburgh and Dundee, and Daimlers for Aberdeen and for Youngs of Paisley. The Aberdeen and Edinburgh examples were on Park Royal frames.

Bruce Coachworks of Cardiff was a subsidiary of East Lancashire Coachbuilders, of Blackburn, and a number of ELC customers took delivery of Bruce bodies, which were built on ELC frames. Bruce built both high- and lowbridge bodies, and not surprisingly, several Welsh operators took delivery of the company's products, including Cardiff (AEC Regent II, III, Bristol KS6G) West Monmouthshire (AEC Regent III, Daimler CVG6), Newport (Leyland PD2) and Green's of Haverfordwest (AEC Regent III). English operators who took Bruce bodies were Eastbourne (AEC Regent III, Crossley DD42, Leyland PD2) and Warrington (Bristol K6G), whilst some BUT 9641T trolley buses were also supplied to Cardiff.

The Loughborough firm of **Brush** was long associated with road passenger transport, having been a supplier of trams in the early part of this century, trolleybuses and their ancillary equipment, and bus bodies. During the war Brush built many austerity bodies, usually on Daimler CW-series chassis, one of the larger customers being London Transport. In the postwar period, Brush returned to supplying those operators that had been its traditional customers, such as Birmingham, Coventry, Derby and Nottingham, the latter also taking trolleybuses with Brush bodies. At the same time Brush also supplied double-deck bodywork to operators such as Bradford, Devon General, Exeter, Gateshead & District, Maidstone, Ribble, Wolverhampton, Yorkshire Woollen and a number of independents. Brush ceased double-deck production around 1950, although the Willowbrook double-deck body of the time had much in common with its Brush counterpart, and many Willowbrook bodies carried plates proclaiming '. . .built under Brush patents'.

It was not unusual, and in fact it still applies today, to find an operator standardising for its bodywork supplies on a local coachbuilder, such a situation long having existed between Blackpool Corporation and H. V. **Burlingham**

Eastbourne Corporation took delivery of eight AEC Regent III in 1951, with these very pleasant looking Bruce bodies, which managed to break away from the look of the East Lancashire Coachbuilders parent, although built on ELC frames.

Later Burlingham bodies featured heavily-radiused windows, as seen here on Salford 453, a 1951 Daimler CVG6, one of four bodied by the Blackpool company.

The bulk of Cravens postwar production went to London Transport on 120 RT chassis. Sheffield, naturally enough, took Cravens bodies – this was one of 15 AEC Regent III of 1949/50.

Ltd, and of course, the local BET operator Ribble was a large customer for Burlingham products. By the end of the 1940s Burlingham had developed a very distinctive double-deck body design, with heavily radiused windows and a raked front, an example of this body on a Daimler CD650 chassis being exhibited in the Transport Hall of the 1951 Festival of Britain exhibition on London's South Bank, the bus subsequently going to Rossie Motors. However, before this design was produced, the company supplied many Leyland PD2s to Blackpool with the distinctive full-fronted centre entrance bodywork, and 15 trolleybuses of this design (but with standard rear platforms) were supplied on BUT 9611T chassis to Portsmouth. In addition to the aforementioned, Burlingham supplied double-deck bodies to Cumberland, The Don, Manchester, Salford, Scout, Scottish Omnibuses, Sunderland District, West Wales and a one-off Guy Arab IV for Wolverhampton in the style of the famous Ribble Leyland PD3s. There were lowbridge bodies on Western SMT Leyland Titan PD3/3s, built to Northern Counties design, whilst rear entrance BUTs went to Manchester and forward-entrance Sunbeams to Reading, the latter later passing to Teesside and lasting until 1971, possibly being the last Burlingham double-deck bodies to be built.

Probably the best-known batch of buses produced by **Cravens** of Sheffield were the 120 bodies built on AEC Regent III 0961RT chassis for London Transport, which were simply the standard Craven product modified for LTE practice with the standard RT windscreen, nearside front wing and route number box in the front dome; being non-standard, these buses only lasted with LT from 1949 to 1956, 119 of them being sold to independents and municipalities. Naturally, Sheffield had a number of Cravens bodies, on AEC Regent III chassis, on which the firm's RT design was based and Alexanders bought 25 bodies on Guy Mark III chassis in 1948.

In Wales D. J. **Davies** of Merthyr Tydfil built a fair number of double-deck bodies. Merthyr Corporation had Bristol and Foden deckers and Burton-on-Trent had some Guy Arab IIIs, all of them with Davies bodies, with the company supplying Cardiff (Guy Arab IV), Newport and St. Helens (both Leyland PD2) with bodies on Park Royal frames.

Although still extant, these days **Duple** builds only luxury coaches and single-deck buses, whereas up to the

mid-1950s the company produced double-deck bodies. Probably the best customer for double-decker Duple bodies was the Red & White group, taking high- and lowbridge bodies on Guy Arab III chassis for its Cheltenham & District, Newbury & District, Red & White and United Welsh subsidiaries. Barton Transport developed a distinctive front-entrance lowbridge body built by Duple that was fitted to the large number of Leyland PD1 chassis that Barton received after the war, and other operators in that part of England favouring Duple double-deckers were W. Gash of Newark, and Skill's of Nottingham, both on Daimler chassis, whilst Scottish Omnibuses had some attractive lowbridge AEC Regent IIIs so bodied. These bodies were built at Duple's Hendon (London) factory, whereas present Duple bodywork is built at the former Burlingham works in Blackpool.

In Ulster, the Belfast firm of **Harkness** supplied over 90% of Belfast Corporation's double-deck requirements, with AEC 664T, BUT 9641T, Guy BTX and Sunbeam trolleybuses, and Daimler CVA6, CVG6 and Guy Arab III motor buses. Back to England and near Bristol were the **Longwell Green** coachworks, and again, although principally concerned with single-deck production, the company did build some double-decker bodies in the late 1950s, and 1960s. Aberdare UDC had some Guy Arab IVs with Longwell Green bodies, whilst Cardiff and Newport took Daimlers. The only significant English customer was Stockport Corporation which took a number of Leyland PD2/40s, some of which lasted into the Greater Manchester Transport era. The last Longwell Green bodies built were mounted on two of the last AEC Regent Vs and supplied to Pontypridd, where they were still running in the spring of 1981, albeit with Taff-Ely. Across the Severn estuary from the Longwell Green works is the village of Lydney, which housed a coachworks that supplied the Red and White group with large numbers of coach and bus bodies. Amongst the double-deckers built by **Lydney** was a number on AEC Regent III chassis for Cheltenham & District and Venture, Basingstoke, which were indistinguishable from the standard Weymann product of the time, on whose frames the bodies were built. The Lancashire municipal operator Leigh took delivery in 1949 of a batch of Lydney lowbridge bodies on Leyland PD2 chassis.

A very popular choice with many municipal operators and also with those independents who purchased new

Left: Duple produced an attractive four-bay body during this period, which had much aluminium beading and embellishment. It is seen here on Scottish Omnibuses BB74, a 1949 AEC Regent III with 53 seats, seen in Glasgow in 1959.

Right: All of Belfast Corporation's postwar deliveries up to 1958 had Harkness bodies, initially built on Park Royal frames, but subsequently using Metal Sections framing. One of the latter, 369, is seen in Donegal Square in 1960.

double-deckers were the products of **Massey** Bros, Pemberton, Wigan, although it was only in later years that Wigan Corporation actually purchased Massey bodies. However, they were long-time favourites with the East Anglian municipal operators, with Colchester (AEC), Great Yarmouth (Leyland) and Ipswich (Ransomes trolleybuses) being prewar customers, postwar deliveries going to Colchester (AEC, Crossley), Great Yarmouth (AEC, Leyland), Lowestoft (AEC, Leyland), Ipswich (AEC) and Southend (AEC, Daimler, Leyland). Other customers were Maidstone, Exeter, Bedwas & Machen, Caerphilly, West Monmouth, Birkenhead, Chester, Newcastle, Cumberland, Barrow, Morecambe, Baxter's of Airdrie, Sunderland, Burnley, Colne and Nelson, Burton, Rowbothams of Harriseahead, Turner's of Brown Edge and Moore's of Kevedon, amongst others. One of the ex-Moore's Massey-bodies buses is here in California, as I saw 20 PVX speeding along the Pacific Coast Highway at Malibu, headed towards Los Angeles painted in red livery, during July 1981. Massey Bros. was taken-over by Northern Counties in the late 1960s.

Before the war, the main customer of **Northern Coachbuilders** Ltd was Newcastle-upon-Tyne Corporation, but in the postwar boom, NCB bodies found favour with a far greater number of operators, with customers as far apart as Scotland and Hampshire, with Hants. and Sussex taking Leyland PD1s with both high- and lowbridge bodies, Aberdeen, and Dundee and Glasgow also taking NCB bodywork. Northern Coachbuilders built trolleybus bodies, including a number to replace war-damaged bodies for London Transport on AEC and Leyland three-axle chassis, and also for Bradford, Maidstone, Newcastle and South Shields. In 1950 a designer from Eastern Coach Works joined the Gateshead company and the NCB double-decker took on a distinct 'Lowestoft' look, including some BUT 9611T trolleybuses for Cleethorpes, that were later sold to Walsall, extended to 30ft length and converted to forward entrance. NCB later concentrated its activities on the building of mobile shops and electric delivery vans. Mention has been made of Duple, which had a one-time subsidiary named **Nudd Bros. & Lockyer,** later to become Duple (Midland) Ltd. However, Nudd Bros. built 60 double-deck bodies on reconditioned Guy Arab II chassis ex-LTE, for Edinburgh Corporation in 1952. These were of the basic Duple design, but featured a full front, the nearside of which was

Lydney built about a dozen double-deck bodies for the Red & White group, when the Cheltenham District, Newbury & District and Venture subsidiaries received some AEC Regents. However, these were built on Weymann frames and looked like Addlestone products.

Originally 95 in the Tynemouth & District fleet was this 1937 AEC Regent I which received a new Pickering 56-seat body in 1949. It is seen here with Gosport & Fareham in 1958, when lunch cost just 2/8d (13p)!

The last double-deck Reading bodies were the two lowbridge 59-seaters supplies on AEC Regent V chassis to West Bridgford UDC in 1958.

unglazed.

So varied were the body styles on offer by **Park Royal** during this period that in an article such as this it is virtually impossible to do justice to the company, added to which the number of operators who took Park Royal bodies on both bus and trolleybus chassis were numerous, both at home and abroad. The largest customer was London Transport with thousands of bodies for the RT, RTL and SRT classes, and the RT influence was very evident in Park Royal designs from 1951-1960.

Another Scottish coachbuilder was **Pickering** of Wishaw, whose products were found mainly in Scotland and north east England, although Brighton, Hove & District had two Guy Arab I chassis with Pickering austerity bodies, these buses later passing to Western National. Perhaps the most famous Pickering double-deck bodies were the streamlined bogie trams supplied to Aberdeen Corporation in 1948. The company also supplied bodies on Albion Venturer chassis to Glasgow, and on AEC and Guy to the Northrn General group.

Another localised supplier of double-deck bodies was the Portsmouth company of **Reading** and Co, whose products were synonymous with the Gosport & Fareham company from prewar days, mainly on AEC Regent, and later, Guy Arab chassis. Portsmouth Corporation took Reading bodies on Leyland PD1 and Crossley chassis, and as the company had supplied many single-deckers to the Channel Islands, it was natural that Jersey Motor Transport should take some Reading double-deckers, on Leyland PD2/20 chassis. Wakes Services, the Somerset independent, had some Reading double-deck bodies, and the only other municipal customer was West Bridgford UDC, with some AEC Regent Vs, possibly the last Reading double-decks built. Back up to Sheffield, and we have **Charles H. Roberts** Ltd, who built a distinctive four-bay double-decker in both high- and lowbridge forms for a number of operators, including Sheffield, Colchester, Liverpool, Nottingham, Accrington, W. Gash, City Coach Co of Brentwood and Griffin, Swansea. Roberts also bodied Sheffield's four-wheel postwar double-deck trams.

In Anglesey, **Saunders Engineering & Shipyard Co.** built bodies at its Beaumaris works, although most of the company's double-deck output was for London Transport's RT programme, with 300 bodies being supplied. Southdown took a good number on refurbished Leyland Titan TD3, TD4 and TD5 chassis, whilst neighbouring

Maidstone & District had 40 Bristol K6A so bodied. In 1951 Saunders produced a lightweight body on an AEC Regent III chassis that was obviously inspired by the RT. Registered OKM 317, the bus demonstrated for a while with M&D, and then went north to Scotland, were it worked with AA Motor Services until very recently. A similar body went on to a 1939 Bristol K5G of Chatham & District. Other purchasers of Saunders bodies were Devon General and Liverpool, although the company will probably be best remembered for bodying the first rear-engined Leyland double-decker, the forerunner of the Atlantean. This was STF 90, which had a four-bay lowheight full-fronted rear entrance open platform body, access to the driver's cab being via a sliding door on the front bulkhead.

Back to London, and by North Acton tube station were the **Strachan's** bodyworks. In prewar days the company was known as Strachan and Brown, being later reconstituted as Strachan's Successors Ltd. In the late 1940s a four-bay double-decker with well-raked frontal profile was produced, which found favour with many independents, particularly in its lowbridge form, although Caerphilly did take some of this configuration on Guy Arab III chassis. In the mid 1950s Strachans introduced a new range of bus and coach bodies, the double-decker reverting to five-bay layout, Moore's Kelvedon taking a number of lowbridge examples whilst Highland Omnibuses had a full-fronted dual-purpose lowbridge Guy Arab III with this body style. Strachans later moved to Hamble, Hants, where a few double-deckers were built, in the mid-1960s.

One of the most popular double-decker bodies was that produced by the Addlestone firm of **Weymann's Ltd,** and apart from supplying many hundreds of bodies for the RT family, the company produced a very well proportioned body, the basic outline of which did not change from 1938 to 1956. Obviously detail changed, with four-bay rubber-mounted windows and other updating modifications, but the profile was unchanged as witness the AEC Regent Vs delivered to Rochdale in 1956. Another interesting point about this Weymann body was that despite the company's involvement with the RT, little of that design was apparent in the standard Weymann body, with the exception of the upper deck emergency exit, which around 1951/2 was restyled in a fashion similar to the RT. Over 40 British concerns took Weymann

Left: Maidstone & District bought 40 Saunders bodies in 1948, mounting them on Bristol K6A chassis. DH223 at Tunbridge Wells.

Right: In 1954 Strachans reverted to a five-bay double-deck design, such as this lowbridge version for Moore Bros, of Kelvedon, on Guy Arab IV.

double-deck bodies in the 10 years 1946-56, including seven trolleybus operators plus a number of foreign companies, particularly in Portugal and South Africa.

A number of operators built their own bodywork during the period, including BMMO, Birch Bros, Brighton Hove & District, Bristol, CIE, Silcox of Pembroke Dock and the Ulster Transport Authority, but of these only **Bristol** supplied other operators, rebodying many wartime Guys for the Red & White group.

Three chassis manufacterers built double-deck bodies **Crossley, Guy** and **Leyland.** Crossley, unlike the other two, supplied bodywork on chassis other than their own, including AEC, Daimler, Guy, Foden and Leyland, and of the three it was the only one to supply trolleybus bodies in this period, with four-wheelers for Ashton and Manchester plus some three-axle examples for the latter. The Guy bodies were of the then standard Park Royal five-bay layout, and were often built on PRV framework, a number of which went for export. Leyland bodywork was the backbone of many fleets and over 70 operators took Leyland Titans with Leyland bodywork.

Although not strictly a builder of bodywork, an article of this nature should mention the Oldham firm of **Metal Sections,** which was for a long time a subsidiary of Tube Investments and is now part of the Duple group. Metal Sections, or MetSec as the company was known, supplied framework for double-deck bodywork, which was used by a number of companies, mostly abroad in Africa; and Hong Kong, but in Belfast, Harkness used MetSec framing and in the Republic of Ireland when CIE bodied its D-class Leyland PDRI Atlanteans, these were again on MetSec frames.

Lack of space prevents more than a passing reference to many of the other double-deck bodybuilders of the time, many of whom found most business from local operators. There was **Ashcroft,** which built Leylands for Birkenhead Corporation in 1954; **Associated Coachbuilders,** with Daimlers for Sunderland the same year; **Barnard,** with customers in Yorkshire and Scotland; **Croft** in Glasgow, mainly supplying local operators; **Mann Egerton** of Norwich, which built a handful of double-deck bodies, two for Sheffield Leylands and one on a Glasgow Daimler; **Scottish Aviation** was another 'occasional' double-deck builder, as was **Welsh Metal Industries,** and both built mainly on Albion and Foden chassis; **Wilkes & Meade** built very few double-deckers, the best known being the three six-bay, full-fronted lowbridge coaches on Daimler chassis for Premier Travel; whilst **Yeates** of Loughborough's sole contribution was a couple of bodies on Leyland PD3 chassis for The Delaine, of Bourne, Lincs.

Left: An example of a local coachbuilder supplying an operator with bodywork, when Sunderland Corporation took delivery of five Daimler CVG5 in 1954 with Associated Coachbuilders 58-seat bodies. These were the only double-deck bodies built by ACB.

Right: Ipswich Borough Transport No 53, a 1963 AEC Regent V with East Lancs body, climbing the hill at Station Street on route 1A to Maidenhall in April 1981, two months before it was withdrawn.

Changes in Ipswich

Photographs by IAN COWLEY

Ipswich 80 was one of its first batch of Willowbrook-bodied AEC Swifts, purchased in 1971. Like other operators, Ipswich experienced reliability problems with Swifts, and these buses are likely to be replaced before older Bristol RELLs.

East Lancs-bodied AEC Swift 90 was one of the first buses to carry the revised livery of darker cream and green. Ipswich single-deckers are mainly confined to the Chantry Estate routes which pass beneath the low Ancaster Road railway bridge.

Leyland Atlantean/Roe 85 was one of the second batch of Atlanteans ordered by Ipswich, and is seen at Cornhill in June 1980.

The prototype Dennis Falcon H, with Duple 51-seat body (Leicester 90) was borrowed by Ipswich, and is seen at Electric House in June 1981. It was the ninth trial vehicle to visit the town since April 1980 as IBT sought replacements for its Regent Vs and unsatisfactory saloons. Six Falcons were subsequently ordered.

The preserved Ipswich AEC Regal IV setting out on the Felixtowe Rally in May 1981. It was one of eight with Park Royal bodies delivered between 1953 and 1955, and which lasted into the early 1970s before being replaced by Reliances and Swifts – now themselves being replaced.

In 1968 Ipswich bought four of these AEC Reliances with Massey 40-seat bodies, and 71 is seen emerging from the archway at the bottom of Lloyds Avenue on a 12A working. The arch has now been closed, because of structural defects. The bus was withdrawn in 1981.

Bickers of Coddenham operates five services from the Debenham area to Ipswich – one of 12 independents operating into the town. This Leyland Leopard, with Marshall 51-seat body, was new in 1968 to Southdown, and was bought from Western National in 1979.

Leaving Ipswich Station on the Clacton-Ipswich service in July 1981 was Eastern National Leyland National 1803. The service is joint with Eastern Counties.

Bigger and Better

Scottish memories from GAVIN BOOTH, sparked off by box camera negatives.

The negatives were still in their original Ilford Films envelopes, complete with the exhortation: 'Bigger and Better – that's how your pictures look when you have enlargements made. It's worth it.' The negatives were 120 size, of pictures taken in my schooldays with a Kodak Box Brownie camera; the price was still written on the envelope – 5/4d (26½p) for developing and printing eight contact-size prints – which tells you that it wasn't yesterday. In fact, the pictures were taken more than 20 years ago, and of my finances at the time had never allowed me to stretch beyond those contact prints.

So I sorted down to a 'short' list of more than 400 negatives, and splashed out on enprints. And in spite of the restrictions of a non-adjustable camera, and sundry subsequent scratches, Ilford was right – the pictures did look better bigger. Not Tom Moore-standard better, you understand, but certainly better. And more important they sparked off many delightful reminders of the varied bus and tram scene that we (some of us, at least) enjoyed then.

A few Scottish memories, then, prompted by the rediscovery of those old box camera pictures.

The giant 1900-bus Alexanders fleet was still whole and undivided in 1960 when this Leyland Tiger TS8 Special was photographed on the Esplanade at Kirkcaldy. There were 105 TS8 Specials, with shortened driving positions to allow 39 seats to be squeezed into the Alexander bodies. They were built in 1939/40, and in 1960 all but half a dozen were still in regular service. P587 was one of the 71 Specials to survive the three-way split of the Alexanders empire in 1961, and worked with Alexanders (Fife) until 1962. But the TS8s were not the oldest buses in the Alexanders fleet when it was split; there were rebodied 1935 TS7s and unrebodied 1936 TD4s, and the longest-surviving examples had 26 years under their belt when eventually withdrawn.

Veterans like P587 were not uncommon in Scotland in 1960. The War and the postwar shortage of suitable vehicles forced Alexanders to get – literally – maximum mileage from its buses, and the company's high maintenance standards undoubtedly helped. But while many of the surviving prewar and wartime buses in other parts of the country were rebodied, or at least heavily rebuilt, most of the older Alexanders buses were unrebodied, and largely in original condition. Sadly, the preservation movement was still in its infancy at the time, and the vast majority of these fine buses went to the breaker's torch.

A giant by 1950 standards, a Belgian-built Bus & Car Eagle from the Continental Trailways fleet, squeezes out of New Street depot in Edinburgh, the principal Scottish Omnibuses depot. New Street is one of the biggest bus garages in Britain, housing at its peak up to 300 buses in its two levels. It also houses the company's head office.

The railway bridge in the left background carries the East Coast main line out of the nearby Waverley Station, and is suitable only for single-deckers, as several drivers have found to their cost, turning right out of New Street with double-deckers.

The 40ft Eagle coach seemed particularly impressive at a time when UK buses could only be 30ft long, and attracted much attention in the depot, and on its exhibition duties, for its was on a tour promoting holidays in the United States. The car on the right is appropriate, but coincidental.

For those seeking interesting independent operators in Scotland, there have always been two Meccas: Paisley and Ayrshire. The situation is still true today, although the disappearance of Patons and Cunninghams in 1979 halved the Paisley attractions.

Not so in Ayrshire, where the long-established and famous co-operative operators, AA, A1 and Clyde Coast, seem to go from strength to strength. And although their buses in the 1980s may be less varied than in the 1950s, they can still offer a greater variety than can be found in many other parts of Britain.

In 1958, the three partners in the AA combine, Dodds of Troon, Youngs of Ayr and Tumilty of Gailes, could muster a fascinating collection of old and new models. Dodds favoured Guys, or Gardner engines at least, while Youngs stuck to Leylands. Tumilty was less obviously selective. This was DGG 910, part of the Dodds contribution, as evidenced by the fleet number DT5; the other partners did not use fleet numbers. The bus, seen at the Boswell Park bus station at Ayr, hub of the AA empire, started life as a 1943 Glasgow Corporation Guy Arab II utility, with Pickering double-deck body, and when withdrawn in 1951, it passed to Dodds after receiving a new Roe centre-entrance 38-seat body, similar to the design supplied at the same time to Darlington Corporation and other operators.

Today there are still two partners in AA, Dodds and Youngs, and there is still evidence of the Gardner/Leyland preferences of the operators. The Ayr-Ardrossan (AA) route remains the main trunk service, and while in the 1950s this was almost exclusively double-deck country, today you are as likely to find single-deckers, like Youngs' Leyland Nationals, complete with Timtronic ticket machines.

When the Alexanders Midland, Fife and Northern companies were created in 1961, there was no immediate external change to the vehicles of the three new companies, other than legal lettering and subtle fleetname changes. In 1962 the new identities were underlined by the adoption of separate liveries; Midland retained the traditional Alexanders azure blue, Fife adopted Tilling-style Ayres red, and Northern a strong, and attractive yellow. All three schemes were relieved by off-white.

The first Northern buses were anxiously anticipated, and along with many of my contemporaries, my first sight of the livery was on an Omnibus Society Scottish Branch tour in June 1962. We had seen a yellow AEC Regal at Blairgowrie, but the main excitement was the prospect of a yellow *double*-decker, which we were told to expect in Dundee bus station. NRB194, a 1958 Leyland Titan PD3/3 with 67-seat Alexander lowbridge body, duly appeared, and a couple of dozen camera shutters clicked simultaneously to record this amazing sight.

While the SMT group spread its network through most of central Scotland and up into the north-east, south-west Scotland was in the hands of a Tilling group company, the Caledonian Omnibus Company of Dumfries. Following nationalisation of the Tilling and SMT groups, Caledonian passed into the hands of the new Scottish Omnibuses group, and Western SMT gained a useful and natural extension to its large empire stretching to the west and south of Glasgow, covering Renfrewshire and Ayrshire.

138 Caledonian buses passed into the Western fleet in 1950, but only four were still to be seen in 1961 when this photograph was taken at Whitesands bus stance at Dumfries. They were oddments in the Western fleet – indeed, oddments in a Scottish fleet – looking like refugees from the Tilling group which, of course, they were. This Bristol K6B, with 55-seat lowbridge Eastern Coach Works body, was one of two delivered to Caledonian in 1948. Alongside, with similar-looking body, was a 1946 AEC Regal with a body actually built by Bristol in 1955.

Glasgow Corporation introduced Britain's last trolleybus system in 1949, and out of 195 vehicles bought, only 21 were single-deckers. The frst was TB35, a 1950 BUT RETB1 with two-door Weymann 27-seat standee body, featuring a conductor's pay desk above the rear axle. In 1953 TB35 became TBS1, and in 1961 it was upseated to 36, and the rear entrance and pay desk were removed. There were ten similar buses, supplied in 1953 with East Lancs bodies; they, too, were rebuilt to single (centre) door layout late in their lives.

In April 1962 TBS1 was hired by the Omnibus Society Scottish Branch for a tour of the already shrinking Glasgow trolleybus network – including a short section between routes on battery power alone. It is seen in Victoria Road on what the Glaswegians call a 'dreich' day. It survived to 1964, and Glasgow's trolleybus system lasted only three more years, to close in May 1967, with its newest double-deckers barely eight years old.

If the Glasgow Corporation trolleybus fleet enjoyed only a brief, and relatively undistinguished, lifespan, Glasgow's trams were quite another matter. This great system ranked among the best in Europe, and in 1937 GCT introduced its superb Coronation cars, big streamlined 64-seat bogie trams, of which 152 were built between 1937 and 1941, and a further six in 1954. 1213, on the left of this 1960 view at the Dalmiur West terminus of service 9, was a 1938 Coronation car, one of 90 delivered in that year – the year of the Empire Exhibition at Glasgow's Bellahouston Park. Alongside is 1320, a Coronation Mk II – better known as a Cunarder; GCT built 100 of these 'caurs' in 1948-52, mostly 70-seaters, with a similar, but slightly more rounded, appearance. Dalmuir West, on the north bank of the Clyde, was the most westerly terminus on the GCT system, and beyond the trams the road leads towards Loch Lomond and the West Highlands. Dalmuir West was also one of the two final tram termini on the Glasgow system, for service 9 was the last to be withdrawn, when the great system finally closed in September 1962.

My local operator, Edinburgh Corporation, had an unsusually large single-deck fleet in the 1950s, a legacy of the 19th century determination of the North British and Caledonian railway companies to strengthen their presences in Edinburgh and Leith by building competing, and often unnecessary, lines all over the city, and leaving future tram and bus operators to cope with more than their fare share of low bridges.

Service 1 was ECT's first proper bus service, started late in 1919, and eventually operated under licence number M1 from the Scottish Traffic Commissioners. It served the populous Easter Road, High Street and Fountainbridge areas of Edinburgh, and eventually extended to serve the later council housing developments at Saughton and Stenhouse, and the old village of Corstorphine. In 1958, every third bus was extended around the north of the city, serving new housing areas and the heart of Leith, to form a complete circle, numbered 21. As the demand for the circular service grew, it was decided that all buses would undertake the full circle, and in 1962 the circle was given the historic 1 number.

For many years the mainstay of the 1 route had been a hard-working batch of prewar Daimlers, some rebodied, but most heavily rebuilt by ECT in the 1948-51 period. To these had been added 35 postwar buses, all with traditionally Scottish cut-away rear entrance bodies. There were Bristol L6Bs, a rare breed in Scotland, Guy Arab IIIs and Daimler CVG5s. One of the Daimlers, 695, new in 1948 with Metro-Cammell 36-seat body, is seen in 1959 pausing for breath after the long climb to the Clermiston layover point. The large Clermiston housing development was one of the reasons for the extension of the 1/21. The ageing single-decks were replaced in 1959-61 by 100 Leyland Tiger Cubs with Weymann bodies, but bridge-heightening and road-lowering meant that in 1966 the 1 Circle could be double-decked.

When this Crossley from the fleet of Smith's of Barrhead was photographed at Paisley Abbey in 1959, it belonged to one of five principal independent operators with services to, or through, Paisley. Three have now gone – Smith's in 1968, and Patons and Cunninghams in 1979, all to the local Scottish Bus Group operator, Western SMT. Grahams and McGills remain today to keep the Paisley independent tradition alive.

Smith's was owned by the Scottish Co-operative Wholesale Society, but like other SCWS-owned fleets, traded under its previous name. The bus seen here is a rare combination for Scotland – where Crossley chassis and Roe bodies were never common, together or apart. It is a 1948 Crossley DD42/5 with lowbridge Roe 53-seat bodywork. The Smith's fleet latterly contained some Leyland Titan PD2s, and four relatively rare AEC double-deckers, two Bridgemasters and two Renowns. None of the Smith's buses was retained by Western SMT.

A Man for all Seasons

MIKE GREENWOOD recalls the last days of the Midland Red D9, the popular own-make 30ft double-deck model built between 1958 and 1966. The D9 class ran to 345 buses, and they were able performers in all weathers.

Midland Red D9 no. 5370 displays the classic lines of this popular type at Scraptoft Lane, Leicester, on a sunny day in July 1979.

Above: More Leicester sunshine, as 5399 leads the charge from Humberstone Gate East in August 1979.

Below: Midwinter between Wanlip and Birstall, and 5362 caught on an overcast day in February 1979.

Leaving a well-camouflaged bus lay-by, 5341 rejoins the main road on its journey to Thurnby Lodge in February 1979.

Basking in the June sunshine in 1979, 5341 is framed between tree and pedestrians.

Night photography is possible throughout the year, although this picture of 5370 was in fact taken in the early morning, late in December 1979.

Invasion from Abroad

ALAN MILLAR

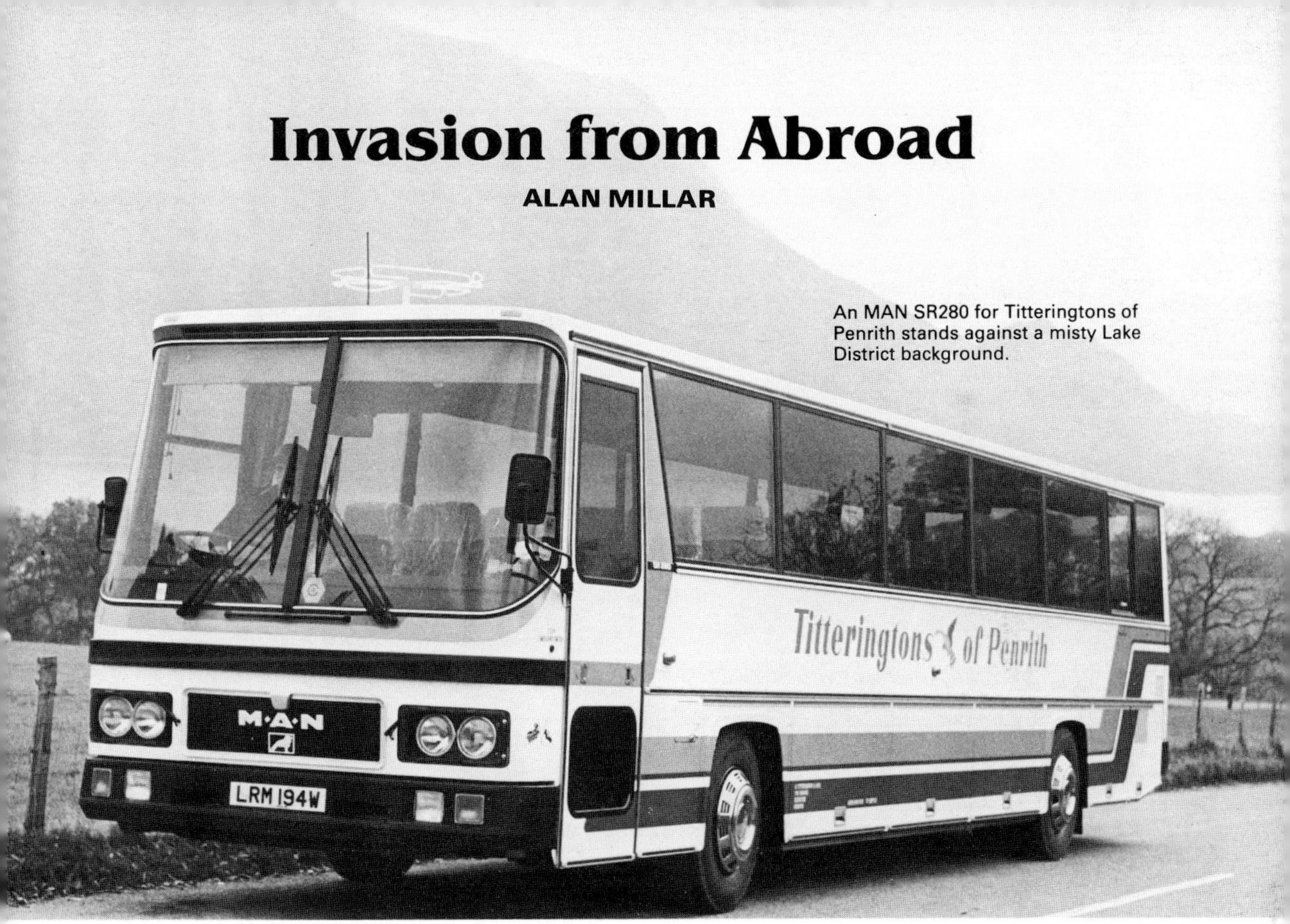

An MAN SR280 for Titteringtons of Penrith stands against a misty Lake District background.

Twenty years ago, you couldn't lay your hands on a foreign built bus or coach in Britain if you tried, yet, in 1980, just over eight per cent of new vehicle sales were of foreign chassis. A year earlier, the figure was only four per cent, and if you eliminate the largely public sector bus market, then the percentage share of imported chassis goes much higher. What has been happening?

It probably has much more to do with a reduction in the choice of British products than it does to British membership of the European Economic Community. Indeed, two of the most successful importers – Volvo and Scania – are based in Sweden, outside the EEC, and Spanish and Portuguese coachbuilders have achieved similar market penetration without the benefit of EEC membership.

By the mid-1960s, rationalisation of home manufacturers' model ranges, together with a mite too much conservatism among the major operators which dominated the industry, meant that the coach operator could buy either a front-engined lightweight or a mid-engined heavyweight, and the service bus scene was swinging headlong into a dangerous monopoly of rear-engined British Leyland double-deckers and rear-engined single-deck city buses. The adventurous coach operator could try Daimler's Roadliner, with Cummins or Perkins rear vee engine, but he probably needed his head examined if he bought any more. There was scope for more choice, and it was not long in coming.

Mercedes-Benz, the German manufacturer which had introduced the first diesel-engined commercial vehicle to Britain in 1928, was first off the mark in the race to change the ways of the country's coach and bus operators. Its 0302 integral coach, fitted with rear-mounted 185bhp diesel as an 11m coach, or 230bhp in 12m form, was descended from a long line of vehicles built for use on autobahns. The mass-produced 0302 came with all-metal integral bodywork, air suspension, exhaust brake, and power-assisted steering, and had been selling at a rate of around 1,600 a year from its introduction in 1965.

A 43-seat 11m prototype right-hand drive model was brought to Britain in 1967, and was registered appropriately OLH 302E. Trials with Scottish Bus Group, Transport Holding Company, and British Electric Traction companies followed, but it was not until June 1968, when the former Ministry of Transport deleted its minimum ground clearance requirements, that Mercedes could obtain a certificate of fitness for the 0302 and start to try and sell it for the then high price of £9,900.

While Whiteford of Lanark bought the prototype, and Seamark's of Luton invested in seven for its London-Luton Airport service, Mercedes found the going heavier than expected. Few doubted the strength and quality of the 0302, but with the Deutschmark rising in value against sterling, there were not many operators who felt they could justify the expense of buying a coach which was not made in Britain.

To try to break down this resistance, and to meet a peculiar British desire for bodywork incorporating timber framing, Mercedes exhibited a Plaxton Panorama Elite-bodied 0302 at the 1969 Scottish Motor Show. The 11m 48-seater was offered for less than the £13,000 then demanded for the all-German version, and the prototype went to World Wide Coaches, which was later to take 13 standard all-German 0302s. A few other models were built for use in Britain, but hindered in particular by the lack of a strong sales force and dealer network, Mercedes' promise of 1968 has never been realised.

The marque made something of a comeback in Britain in 1978, when it sold 25 Plaxton-bodied 0303 models, successors to the 0302,to the newly-established London branch of Wahl Coaches, a West German enterprise. But, only two 0303s were sold in Britain in 1979, and only one the following year, and Wahl has found that lightweight Bedfords meet many of its London requirements. Indeed, Wahl found it necessary to sell some of its 0303s in South Africa where Mercedes has done rather better.

Mercedes was called in by Selnec PTE in 1973, when it wanted to test a European city bus against other single-deckers then being introduced into its fleet. It specified two 0305 rear-engined underframes with 170bhp engines, three-speed torque converter automatic transmissions, and pneumatic suspension, and had Northern Counties single-deck standee bodies built for them to its own design. No more were built, but three 0305G left-hand drive articulated buses, with French bodywork assembled by Lex Engineering, in Hampshire, entered service on the tarmac at Luton Airport in 1981.

Mercedes' failure in Britain contrasts sharply with the notable, if rather spasmodic, success achieved by Scania, the Swedish manufacturer which launched an assault on the British bus market late in 1969. After two years in which it sold around 1,000 lorries in Britain, the company reached an agreement with Metro-Cammell Weymann to build a range of BR111 single-deck citybuses and market them in Britain as Metro-Scanias.

With its low-floor integral construction body, 11 litre rear-mounted diesel, air suspension, and torque converter automatic transmission, the Scania represented a significant advance over the generally poor rear-engined single-deckers available in Britain, and it was a sound

Left: A World Wide Mercedes-Benz 0302 at Ludlow, in Shropshire.

Right: One of two Metro-Scania single-deckers operated by Merthyr Tydfil alongside Leyland Nationals and Bristol REs.

alternative to the Leyland National once it became available in 1971. The body followed Scania design closely, but one worthwhile MCW innovation was a deeper nearside windscreen intended to improve kerbside visibility.

Leicester was an enthusiastic supporter of the Metro-Scania, taking 35 examples, and Newport, unable to obtain delivery of British vehicles in time, bought 44 in 1971/72 as part of a programme of converting all of its services to one-man operation. In all, 133 vehicles were built, but by 1973 the demand for single-deck city buses had fallen sharply, and MCW and its Swedish partner were working on a double-deck version, the Metropolitan.

This shared the running gear of its single-deck predecessor, but the bodywork was of a much more British style, modelled on the designs supplied to the PTEs and London Transport. It came on to the market at the time when Leyland's delivery and service back-up record for its Atlantean, Fleetline, and VRT had hit an all-time low, and when new bus grant was pushing up the demand for new vehicles. The result of this was that, even before the Metropolitan was officially unveiled in October 1973, an unprecedented volume of orders had been placed for it.

A five-year production run followed, with pride of place being taken by a 164-vehicle order from London Transport, which already had six Metro-Scania single-deckers and which was embarking upon an urgent replacement programme involving its fleet of late-1960s AEC Merlins. Initial enthusiasm from such quarters as Leicester (68 buses), Merseyside (60) and West Yorkshire PTEs (95) waned, but Tyne and Wear showed faith to the extent of taking 140 and Reading bought 33. MCW managed even to export two, to Hong Kong's China Motor Bus company, and 660 in all went to British customers.

Unfortunately, the industry's expectations for the Metropolitan generally exceeded its capabilities, and it was let down by heavy fuel consumption, over-lively suspension, an exceedingly complex and not very reliable gearbox, inadequate spares back-up from MCW, and by serious corrosion problems caused by the use of steel framing and aluminium panels together in the body construction. Sadly, some of LT's fleet had already gone to the breaker's yard by 1980.

MCW soon realised that all was not well, and set about developing an all-British bus, using lessons learnt from the Metropolitan, and this emerged in 1978 as the Metrobus, with which it has had rather more success both at home and overseas.

Scania, though, was not going to take defeat lying down, and in 1980 it re-entered the British double-deck market with its BR112DH, a semi-integral chassis

designed specifically for Britain, but incorporating running units from its BR112 single-deck range. To counter criticism of the Metropolitan's gearbox, this was offered with a Voith gearbox or an improved design of Scania transmission, and the company insisted that its fuel consumption was superior to the earlier model. Scania UK had already taken over responsibility for spare parts distribution for the MCW vehicles, with noticeable improvements for operators.

With a chassis price of £25,000 – significantly lower than that for any British chassis – Scania was determined to win itself orders for around 150 buses a year. That was the theory. It did not allow for a recession in the economy from the spring of 1980, and its consequent effects on operators' patriotism. Apart from 11 Marshall-bodied examples for Newport's virtually all-Scania fleet, and experimental examples for Tyne and Wear and Greater Manchester PTEs, it has failed to win business in a shrinking market served by four British manufacturers offering seven different models.

One other Scania model was imported in 1973, but its fate was similar to that of the Mercedes-Benz 0302. Based on the Scania CR145, the 14.2 litre V8-engined Metro-Scania 37-seater luxury coach was modelled closely on Swedish designs, but had British Self Changing Gears transmission. It was tested by National Travel at a time when it was planning to invest in high quality coaches for the then new white coach network. Unfortunately, the plans for high quality coaches did not get any further forward than the Scania coach.

Volvo, the other Swedish commercial vehicle giant, adopted a very different approach to the British market, due largely to the vision and showmanship of its importer, former haulier Jim McKelvie. Having built up Ailsa Trucks as a highly successful importing and sales organisation for Volvo F86 and F88 lorries, McKelvie turned his attention to Volvo's bus and coach range, and established Ailsa Bus Ltd to sell B58 coaches and B59 city buses.

The first B58, fitted with SCG semi-automatic transmission and Alexander Y-type body to Scottish Bus Group specification, was completed in 1972, and entered trial service with Eastern Scottish in January 1973. This model was made for the British market, if anything ever was. Its mid-mounted 230bhp turbocharged engine combined the familiarity of British designs with the

Left: One of the Bedford-engined Caetano integral coaches imported by Moseley.

Right: Dodds of Troon bought this Bedford YMT with Jonckheere Bermuda body, in 1977.

additional power of a Volvo, and it soon established a niche for itself, especially when offered with a synchromesh gearbox.

Sales began to fall around 1977, but new management at Ailsa, by then under Volvo's control (and later renamed Volvo Bus), strengthened the dealer network and increased the company's sales effort. As a result, 98 B58s were sold in 1978, 216 in 1979, and it sold 393 coaches (and a few service buses) in Britain in 1980.

The company found that, with an increasing demand for heavy duty coaches, it was winning hands down against Leyland which, at that time, was phasing out its AEC Reliance model, and was unable to meet the demand with the less powerful Leopard. The B58 specification was improved to include optional air-overleaf suspension and Allison automatic transmission, and in 1980 it was replaced by the B10M model which incorporates full air suspension.

B59 sales were not just disappointing, they did not happen at all. A British prototype, with 230bhp underfloor rear engine and two-door Marshall Camair semi-integral body, was exhibited at the 1972 Commercial Motor Show, and underwent trials the following year. But, for all its excellence and its success in other markets, the demand for such buses in Britain had passed its peak, and the prototype was destined to lead an ignominious life in the service of remote Scottish independents. Volvo's penetration of the bus market was left to the Ailsa, a front-engined double-decker designed and built in Scotland, using mainly British components.

Volvo's success with the B58 prompted DAF to have a similar go with its MB200 model. There were several similarities in this case, as the Dutch manufacturer had already established itself as a highly successful lorry importer into Britain, and its coach, like the Volvo, was a conventional mid-engined machine. A prototype, with Duple Dominant body, was delivered to Robinson's of Appleby in 1975, and business had grown to a total of 12 sales in 1978.

Another 20 were sold in 1979, by which time a 251bhp turbocharged model was being imported, and DAF announced plans for a 110 vehicle assault on the British market, with 85 MB200 and 25 SB2000 semi-integral rear-engined coaches incorporating a 230bhp 8.25 litre charge-cooled vertical engine. While it only sold 48 coaches in 1980, almost all of them MB200s, it has lost

none of its grip on the market, and like Volvo, has filled some of the vacuum created between the end of Reliance production and the launch in 1981 of Leyland's high-powered Tiger.

The SB2000, with which DAF has had some teething troubles in Britain, offers superior luggage accommodation as well as the greater rigidity of the integral body construction. But many of its features began to be available to British operations from 1981 when a smaller Dutch manufacturer, Bova, began to sell its DAF-powered rear-engined integral coaches through the Moseley Group at the highly attractive price of £49,000 – how inflation has taken root since 1968!

South Yorkshire PTE's enthusiasm for articulated buses forced it to look outside Britain for vehicles, with the result that five West German MAN – Maschinenfabrik Augsburg Nurnberg – models were brought to Sheffield in 1978/79, ready for the launch of scheduled articulated bus services in the summer of 1979. Five Leyland-DABs, built by Leyland's Danish subsidiary, were also imported and bodied at the Leyland National factory, and were followed by similar, Roe-bodied vehicles for British Airways.

MAN followed this almost accidental arrival on the British market with the launch, later in 1979, of a British version of its integral rear-engined SR280 coach. This 280bhp high specification coach really turned the clock back to 1968, and Mercedes' arrival on the scene, but the company's preparedness to offer substantial discounts on the purchase price for the SR280, presumably with the intention of making a higher profit from spare parts sales, and a more convincing sales effort guaranteed the sale of its entire British quota of 25 coaches in 1980. Continued success in 1981 prompted Duple, as bodybuilder to Leyland, Volvo and DAF, to offer a high-floor coach body for the 1982 season, largely to provide the level of comfort and luggage accommodation available on the SR280 and Bova.

The 1980 Motor Show also was the point of introduction of two other West German integral designs to the British market. Kässbohrer exhibited a Mercedes-powered HD215 rear-engined vehicle destined for Kirkby's of Rayleigh, Essex, and the first legendary Neoplan coach for a British operator, ironically for Blueways of London to carry the English football team, appeared from Gottlob Auwärter, of Stuttgart.

The Neoplan range of two and three-axle high-floor and

Far left: A Volvo B10M with high-floor Van Hool Alizee body.

Left: Mercedes' British renaissance came in 1978 with the supply of Plaxton-bodied 0303s to Wahl Coaches, of London. The bodies incorporated Mercedes front ends, to good effect.

Overleaf, top: Memories of two of the many coachbuilders that once produced double-deck bodies, from 1950 advertisements. The Burlingham body was one of 15 built on BUT 9611T trolleybus chassis for Portsmouth Corporation in 1950/51. The Bruce body was one of 14 built for Warrington Corporation in 1947/48 on rare Bristol K6G chassis.

Overleaf, bottom: Two more names from the ranks of vanished bodybuilders, represented by contemporary advertisements. The 1953 Crossley ad shows an Oldham Corporation all-Crossley DD42/8. Roberts of Wakefield shows two Scottish buses in this 1950 ad, a 1949 Foden PVSC6 with 35-seat body for Strachans Deeside Omnibus Service, of Ballater, and a Glasgow Corporation Albion Venturer CX37S, one of 40 supplied in 1949.

double-deck coaches had already become familiar to British eyes, as these glass and steel galleons transported continental tourists arounds the obligatory attractions of London and the rest of Britain. Blueways' vehicle was a two-axle Mercedes-powered Cityliner 12m coach, but the first right-hand drive three-axle 70-seat Skyliner double-deckers for a British operator went into service in autumn 1981 on Trathen of Yelverton's London-Plymouth Rapide service. These £120,000 coaches, powered by 360bhp Mercedes V10 engines, are the forerunners of more Neoplan coaches being imported by the company's British agents.

Just as the reduction in the number of British chassis helped prompt a European invasion, so has the streamlining of the coach bodybuilding industry.

Moseley went to Portugal from 1968 for Salvador Caetano coachwork which, while marginally tasteless to some British eyes, offered a bright alternative to Duple and Plaxton bodies on standard British chassis. A few Caetano rear-engined integral coaches, with Bedford YRQ running units, were imported in 1974, and Moseley also brought in a handful of AEC-UTIC rear-engined integrals built by AEC's Portuguese agent and incorporating British units.

Van Hool began to market its coach bodies in Britain from 1970, and had built up its sales considerably by the time its ill-fated Dublin factory was supplying British coach and bus operators in 1976. The Belgian company's Zaragossa factory in Spain, and its main works at Antwerp have taken up where Dublin failed and a measure of its successful penetration of the market must surely be Leyland's specification of one of its Alizée bodies for a Tiger demonstrator.

After a shaky start in the early 1970s, another Belgian coachbuilder, Jonckheere, has established a British sales organisation, and similar moves, with equal success, have been made by Irizar, from Spain's Basque region, and Padane, an Italian company which might yet push Mercedes-Benz 0303 sales into respectable numbers.

The much wider choice of vehicles available to British operators has prompted home manufacturers to strike back with better products. All that remains to be seen is whether Britain can achieve similar European market penetration with models like the Tiger or high-floor Duple coach. It's the least they can do.

BURLINGHAM

Bodies of Distinction

52-SEATER DOUBLE-DECK HIGHBRIDGE TYPE TROLLEY BUS BODY OF METAL FRAME CONSTRUCTION, ONE OF A CONTRACT FOR THE CITY OF PORTSMOUTH

H. V. BURLINGHAM LTD

Motor Body Builders

PRESTON NEW ROAD · BLACKPOOL

Tel: Marton 251-2-3

The "East Lancs" Steel Framed Body by

BRUCE COACH WORKS, LTD.

SOUTH PARK ROAD

Telephone – CARDIFF – 44461/2/3

(IN ASSOCIATION WITH EAST LANCASHIRE COACHBUILDERS LTD., BLACKBURN)

One of 27 Double Deck Steel Framed Bodies now being supplied to

WARRINGTON CORPORATION TRANSPORT DEPARTMENT

Chassis by Messrs Bristol Tramways and Carriage Company Ltd.

CROSSLEY COACHWORK

ALL TYPES OF SINGLE AND DOUBLE DECK OMNIBUS AND TROLLEY BUS BODIES. COACH BODIES. METAL OR COMPOSITE CONSTRUCTION FOR ALL CHASSIS FOR HOME OR ABROAD

Specifications and details gladly sent on request

CROSSLEY MOTORS LIMITED

AN A.C.V. COMPANY

ERRWOOD PARK · STOCKPORT

35-seater Composite Single Deck Coach for Strachans' Services.

Coachwork by

ROBERTS

WAKEFIELD

ESTABLISHED 1856

56-seater normal height metal framed double deck Omnibus body on Albion chassis, for Glasgow Corporation.